NO MAN'S LAND

CELEBRATION OF OPENING OF THE MUSEUM AT FORT JESUP—1959.

NO MAN'S LAND

A History of El Camino Real
by
Louis Raphael Nardini

A FIREBIRD PRESS BOOK

PELICAN PUBLISHING COMPANY
Gretna 1998

Manufactured in the United States of America

Published by Pelican Publishing Company, Inc.
1000 Burmaster Street, Gretna, Louisiana 70053

To
Orine Inez

ACKNOWLEDGMENT

In acknowledging the sources of information and the assistance of the many persons I consulted in the preparation of this book, the author wishes to thank the following: The staffs of the Sabine Parish, the Natchitoches Parish and the Northwestern State College Libraries — with especial thanks to Miss Catherine Bridges who so patiently and ably assisted me in gathering data for this writing. Acknowledgment is gratefully and appreciatingly given to those excellent authors and their publishers listed in the bibliography at the back of this book, for it was through their talent and efforts that a whole new experience was opened to me.

I must remember too my History Teacher, Mrs. Lucille Roy Caffery, who so thoroughly planted in my mind the desire to read and study History, for it was she who told me, "It is the History and the Present which foretells the Future."

I am likewise grateful to Miss Margie Harrison and Mrs. Mabel Fletcher Harrison who corrected and typed this book and to Mrs. Bernice A. Authur of Many, La., who also assisted in the typing of this manuscript.

Louis R. Nardini

PREFACE

There are two ways to write the history of an area. First, the actual-fact-data way, which gives dates, important events and the names of the leaders. But this does not fully explain the reasons for their occurrence, nor show the effect of mass participation. It omits many of the names of others involved in the incident or incidents, so that a clear picture of all the people involved is lacking. Even while one is reading, he is conscious of a mass effect and realizes that a sort of team is present. He then stops and asks himself, "Who were the others?"

The second way is to combine the legends and folklore with the actual fact-data of an area and to use reason and imagination — to seek out the names of others connected with the adventure. Those who went their way, but most important, those who remained to establish, fortify and settle, and by their so doing, give permanence and purpose to the area.

By using the second method, the writer believes he has given a true history of the locality of which he writes, because he has used the actual-fact-data of the area, and added to it the economic and social life of the people involved, especially of those who remain to become inhabitants.

To write a history of such an area as that which includes Natchitoches, El Camino Real, Los Adais and the Neutral Strip, one must be blessed with the knowledge of several languages, and feel that he can comprehend the nature of the people, who for nearly three and one half centuries have passed before him, from the time of Cabeza De Vaca in the year 1530 to the establishment of Fort Jesup by General Zachary Taylor in 1823. One must specially be familiar with the Adais Indians, who were a branch of the great Caddo Federation of Indians and their Nation when Cabeza De Vaca visited the Adais.

At Los Adais an incident occurred which changed the social life of the wilderness frontier. Two sets of Latin eyes met; in them reflected desire, passion, and love. Out of the distance, on a pine-scented wind, came the singing voice of a Spanish serenader, accompanied by the soft music of a string instrument, a bright sun to cause light on shade and in the shade Spanish and French lips met and arms entwined.

A half-naked savage lurks in the shadows nearby. Entranced by the magic of this moment, he speaks and the spell is broken. To the Senorita in Spanish and to the Frenchman in French; "Come, it is time to go." What kind of Indian is this, who speaks both French and Spanish fluently? Only Dachiacoin of the Adais could do this and because of it he ranged far and wide in both the French and Spanish Territories. Dachiacoin had this to say to Padre Certa, "A man needs only one wife, the right one for him, and the woman needs only one husband, the right one for her."

For over fifty years Los Adais was the Capital of the Texas Country and the end of El Camino Real. Here anything was expected to happen and usually did.

El Camino Real, The Royal Road, The King's Highway, The Contraband Trail, The Old San Antonio Trace, The Old Texas Trail, and, lastly, Louisiana Highways 6 and 21 through Texas. This Southland's busiest highway served the outlaw, the murderer, the slave trader, and the priest, as well as the sinner. Regardless of which direction one traveled he had to pass the Adais and the Neutral Strip — this area so filled with love, hate, jealousy, generosity, selfishness, prosperity, and despair. If at all this be possible, then this was El Camino Real, Los Adais and the Neutral Strip.

Because:

The Buffalo migrated southward through Texas and then to Louisiana, following the same trail in the winter of each year. Then the powerful Caddo Nation split and each group followed a leader. The Adais came to settle along this Buffalo Trail near Spanish Lake. El Campti originated the meeting place on the great Sand-bar near Campti, Louisiana, so that each fall of the year all tribes of the Caddo Confederacy could come and trade. Francois Hidalgo desired to establish Missions and settlements to bring more freedom and prosperity to his people and to bring the teaching of the Catholic Faith to all savages of the Tejas country. He wrote a letter to the French Governor of Louisiana, using the pretext of trade as bait.

Results:

The Trading Post at Natchitoches established; the Missions established.

The French Post St. Jean Baptiste, the Spanish Presidio, Del Neustra Senora del Pilar de Los Adais. Both Nations now had to maintain these outposts to prevent encroachment from the other.

Effected:

The desire of both Nations to populate this Frontier. When Mexico won her independence from Spain the Neutral Strip was formed. This lawless unpoliced strip of land became the back door of the United States. Because of this ruthless lawlessness Fort Jesup was established.

The independent spirit of the settlers along the El Camino Real and their desire for freedom resulted in the establishment of the State of Texas.

As I lolled one summer's day beneath an oak near the ruins of Post St. Jean Baptiste des Natchitoches and closed my eyes to give my fancy free play, I thought I heard sounds of all kinds, sounds that had undoubtedly resounded down the years. Could that squealing be the swine of the De Soto adventurers or the shriek of automobile tires coming to a braked stop? Is that rumble I hear that of thundering herds of buffalo or the approach of a diesel locomotive with its long train of cars? Those drums, are they the drums of the Caddo Indians or the drums of a marching high-school band? The whistling roar that reaches my ears, is it a jet plane or the swishing, whistling wings of diving ducks?

Awakened to reality I began the research and study that enabled me to write this book.

CONTENTS

		Page
Preface		IX
Chapter I	El Camino Real	1
II	Some Early History	4
III	Dachicoin — A Noble Indian — Los Adais, 1723	33
IV	St. Denis and the Spanish	42
V	Doctors and Early Medicine — 1722 to 1744	45
VI	Romance at Los Adais	51
VII	Incidents of the Years, 1735-1742	60
VIII	The Three Cabins	63
IX	After St. Denis	74
X	After the Louisiana Purchase	80
XI	The Devil's Play Ground	83
XII	Satan's Agent — John A. Murrell	89
XIII	The Break-up of the Neutral Strip	92
XIV	The Filibuster of 1812-1821	95
XV	Fort Jesup	103
XVI	Texas and Independence, 1831-1836	116
Addenda		
	Land Grants	129
	St. Denis' Family Tree	137
	Baptismal Records of Natchitoches, 1734-1740	138
	Soldiers in Natchitoches — 1742	141
	Merchants, Farmers, Traders in Natchitoches, 1742	142
Reference Bibliography		145
Personalities		149

LIST OF ILLUSTRATIONS AND MAPS

Celebration of the Opening of the Museum
at Fort Jesup, 1959..Frontispiece

Map Showing Locations of Members of Caddo
Indian Federation XV

Map of El Camino Real from Mexico City to Natchitoches.....................XVI

Hinta-sak — a Caddo house.. 8

Hinta-sak — top view showing construction..................................... 9

Plan of Fort at Natchitoches, 1733.. 17

Plan of La Presidio Nuestra Senora de los Delores, 1716........................ 19

Mission of San Miguel De Cuellar De Los Adais, 1717............................. 21

Map Showing Location of Mission and Presidio of
San Miguel De Cuellar De Los Adais... 22

Plan of Presidio De San Antonio De Bexar....................................... 24

Plan of Fort Del Pilar De Los Adais.. 26

La Presidio Nuestra De Senora Del Pilar De Los Adais........................... 28

Map of Natchitoches by Breutin, 1722... 30

Map Showing Neutral Strip.. 87

Map of Fort Jesup Defense Area... 102

Map of the Buildings of Fort Jesup.. 107

Map of Area Around Camp Sabine, 1836... 113

Old Ambroise Sompayrac House at Natchitoches............................ 124

WRAP AROUND

Fort St. Jean Des Natchitoches...Opposite Page 116

Old Kitchen at Fort Jesup...   "   "   117

Officers' Quarters at Fort Jesup—Reproduction.................   "   "   132

Original Plans of Fort Jesup..   "   "   133

Officers' Quarters—Another view..   "   "   133

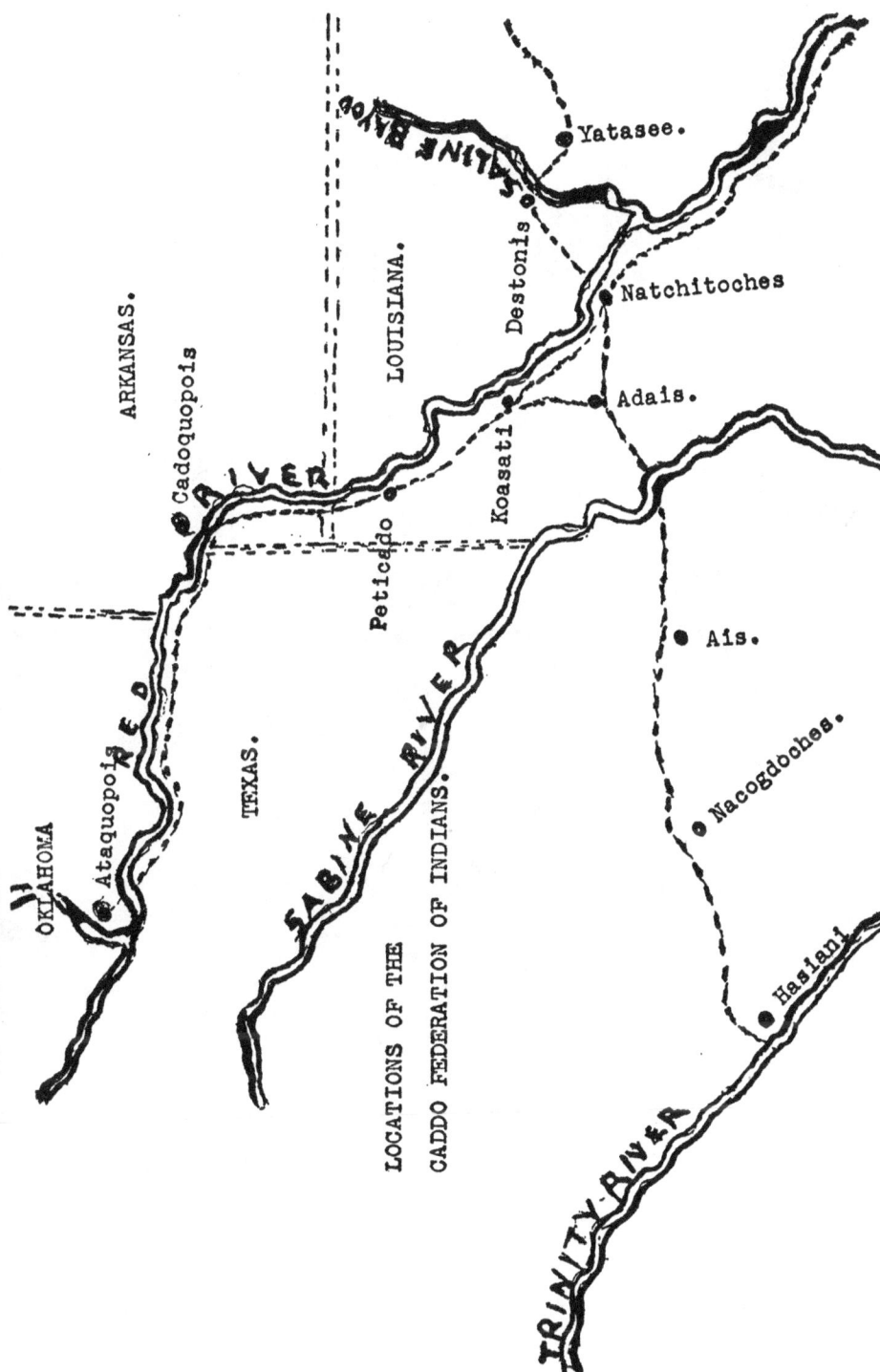

LOCATIONS OF THE
CADDO FEDERATION OF INDIANS.

TEXAS

LOUISIANA.

MEXICO.

GULF OF MEXICO

RED RIVER
SABINE RIVER
NECHES RIVER
TRINITY RIVER
BRAZOS RIVER
COLORADO RIVER
SAN ANTONIO
MEDINA RIVER
NUECES RIVER
RIO SABINAS
RIO GRANDE

NATCHITOCHES
ROBELINE
RED RIVER
ANGELINA RIVER
NACOGDOCHES
SAN REAL
EAGLE PAZAS
MONCLOVA
LAMPAZOS

EL CAMINO REAL

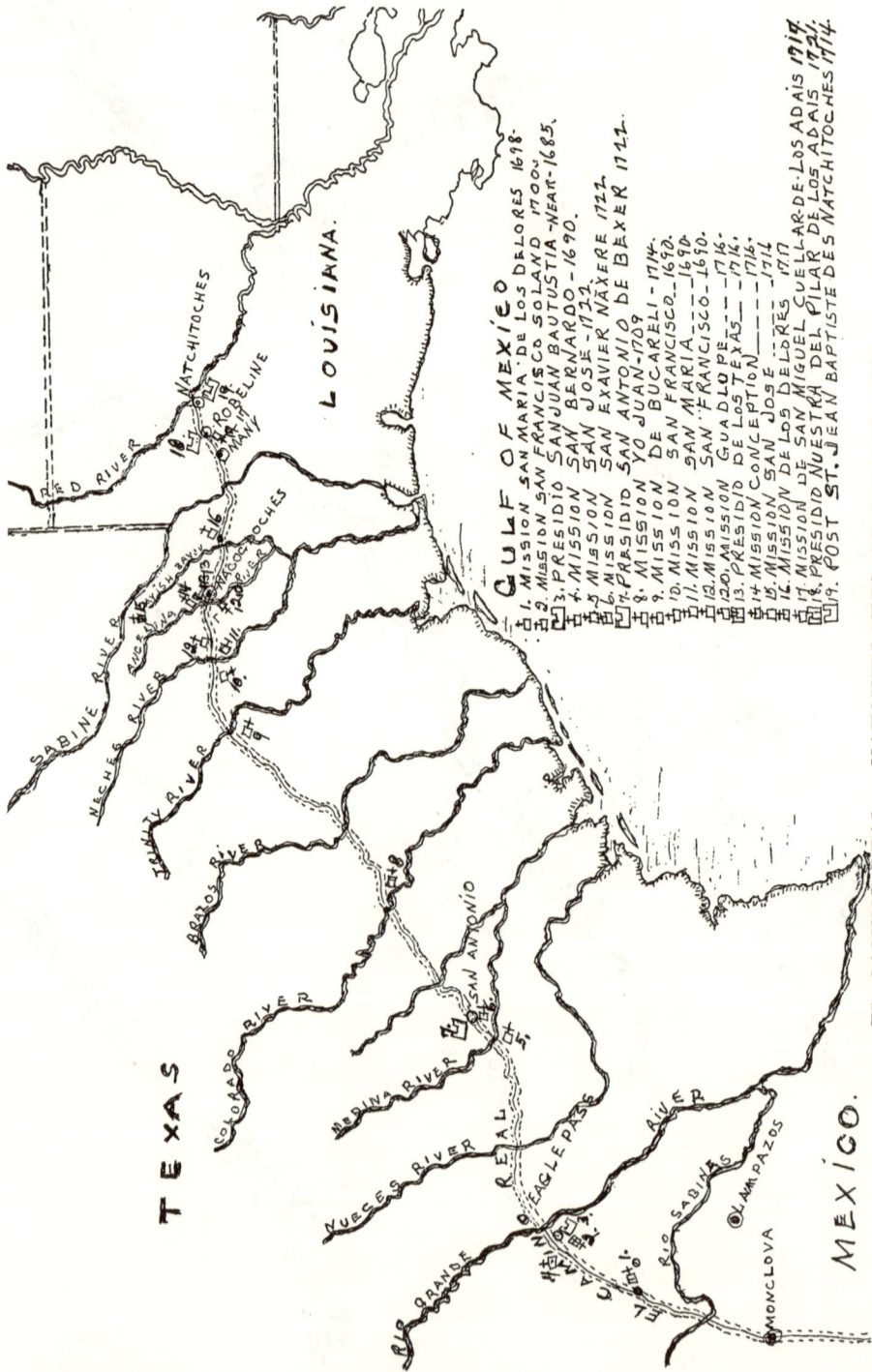

1. Mission San Maria de los Dolores 1698.
2. Mission San Francisco Soland 1700.
3. Presidio San Juan Bautistia - near 1685.
4. Mission San Bernardo - 1690.
5. Mission San Jose 1722.
6. Mission San Exavier Náxere 1722.
7. Presidio San Antonio de Bexer 1722.
8. Mission Yo Juan 1709.
9. Mission de Bucareli 1714.
10. Mission San Francisco 1690.
11. Mission San Maria 1690.
12. Mission San Francisco 1690.
13. Presidio de Los Texas — 1716.
14. Mission Conception — 1716.
15. Mission San Jose — 1714.
16. Mission de los Delos — 1717.
17. Mission de San Miguel Cuellar-de-los Adais 1717.
18. Presidio Nuestra del Pilar de los Adais 1721.
19. Post St. Jean Baptiste des Natchitoches 1714.

EL CAMINO REAL — NATCHITOCHES TO MEXICO CITY

I

EL CAMINO REAL

Each fall of the year the buffalo came out of the Great Plains through Oklahoma and into Texas. At the Trinity River in Texas many of these herds turned eastward to cross the Sabine River into Louisiana, to travel ever eastward and to cross the Red River in the Natchitoches area. The buffalo, being a heavy beast, left a well-marked trail from the Trinity River to the Red River in the Natchitoches area. The buffalo trail now became part of the Caddo Indian Trail system. And later it became El Camino Real.

In Spanish, the words "El Camino Real" mean "The King's Road." That is the exact translation of these words. In Spain, even before the time of the discovery of America, there were several roads or highways listed as El Camino Real. All roads leading to the city in which the King of Spain resided were known as El Camino Real. Actually, the meaning to the Spanish people of the words "El Camino Real" meant *The Road to the King*, hence El Camino Real, *The King's Road*. So here in America when Mexico was conquered and settled by the Spaniards and Mexico City came into being, expeditions were sent out to conquer this new land for the King of Spain. In all directions from Mexico City, Ranchos, Missions and Presidios were established and all roads leading from these establishments back to Mexico City—to the Viceroy, who was the direct representative of the King—were called El Camino Real because these roads led to the Viceroy who was actually the King and Ruler of this New Country.

This El Camino Real, which we in Louisiana and Texas are interested in, began in Mexico City and ended at the "Old Darkey" Statue, at the North end of Front Street in the City of Natchitoches, Louisiana. Some say that El Camino Real begins in San Antonio, Texas, and ends in Natchitoches, Louisiana. I believe this is wrong because the very name of the Road, "El Camino Real, the Road to the King," bears out my theory. I will explain: if one left Natchitoches (I speak of the time when Louisiana was under Spanish domination) and wished to go to the King by El Camino Real, or to the one who directly represented the King in this new country, he would have had to travel to Mexico City and there tell his troubles to the Viceroy, the direct representative of the King of Spain. This would have been between the years 1762 when France gave Louisiana to Spain, and ten years later when Los Adais was abandoned and the site of government moved to Natchitoches, thus filling in the last gap on the Road now known as El Camino Real, (the section of road from Los Adais near Robeline, Louisiana to Natchitoches). Until the year 1762 Los Adais was the site of Government of the "Tejas," or "Texas Country." This area extended from the Presidio Del Norte, as the French called this Spanish Outpost on the Rio Grande River, or El Presidio San Juan Bautista, as it was known to the Spanish. Now, let us pick up the traveler again who had business with the King, past Los Adais, Nacogdoches, San Antonio, the Presidio Del Norte, Saltillo and Queretaro and then to Mexico City and the Viceroy, whose word was final on all matters concerning the Government and the people, and, of course, that covered everything.

THE CADDO FEDERATION OF INDIANS

The southeastern part of Oklahoma, the southwestern part of Arkansas, the Northwestern half of Louisiana and the Northeastern part of Texas was Caddo land, and claimed by the Caddos as their hunting ground. The Caddos were traders and developed trade-routes. Many of the highways of today follow the Caddo trails of yester-year, such as El Camino Real, that portion from the Trinity River in Texas to Natchitoches, Louisiana.

When the Caddo Nations split they settled themselves as follows:

1. The Attaquopois, at the confluence of the Kiamechi River and the Red River in southern Oklahoma.
2. The Caddoquopois or Caddo proper remained on the Red River near Fulton, Arkansas.
3. The Peticaddo on Caddo Lake near Shreveport, Louisiana.
4. The Koasatti near Coushatta, Louisiana.
5. The Destonies on Saline Bayou near Winnfield, Louisiana.
6. The Yatasse on Nantanchie Lake near Montgomery, Louisiana.
7. The Natchitoches on the Red River at Natchitoches, Louisiana.
8. The Adais near Robeline, Louisiana, on a large lake now called Spanish Lake.
9. The Ais at San Augustine, Texas.
10. The Nacogdoches at Nacogdoches, Texas.
11. The Hasinai consisting of four tribes on the Trinity River in Texas, referred to by the Spanish as the Tejas (some historians classify them as Caddos. They spoke the Caddo language).

The Ais Indians had as their neighbors to the west the Hasinai federation of Indians which was composed of four tribes: The Nacogdoches at Nacogdoches; the Bidais, the Nasoni and the Nabidache, the latter three were located on the Trinity River.

Such was the situation when the first aliens came in contact with the Caddos.

II

SOME EARLY HISTORY

In his book, "La Relacion que Dio Alvar Nunez Cabeza De Vaca delo Acaescido unlas Indias", De Vaca writes in the year 1530 that "we were among the Adayes (Adais), the others were Juan Castillo, Andrea Dorantes and Estabancio of Azmor who was a slave of Dorantes. These four survivors were of 300 of the Panfilio Narvez expedition that went into Florida in 1528.

Narvez's expedition, beaten by the Apalache Indians, unable to return to their ships, killed their horses, ate the meat, used the hides to make bellows and water casks; they forged their armor and weapons to make tools and nails, then constructed four boats. They skirted the coasts of Alabama, Mississippi and Louisiana, foraging for food. During a storm the boats were wrecked, four survived to become slaves of the coastal Indians.

De Vaca and his companions became traders and medicine men. Meanwhile they learned to live off the land as the Indians did. They planned and successfully escaped . . . And now they were among the Adais seeking directions. They were the first white men to travel westward over the Buffalo Trail. They wandered ever westward and finally found a Spanish patrol from Mexico.

De Vaca was the only one of the three hundred to return to Spain and even before he published his book in 1542, he had inspired the Hernando DeSoto expedition into Florida with his story of the City of Cibola, a city built entirely of gold.

Hernando DeSoto, the Golden Eagle, led the next expedition into Florida. Continuously harassed by the Appalachie tribes of

Indians of the southeastern states he crossed the Mississippi and now in the year 1540 he marched into Louisiana, pillaging, raping and destroying. He was assisted by these trusting Lieutenants: Don Luis Moscoso, Don Juan de Anasco, Don Baltazarde Gallegardo, Don Juan Labillo, Don Carlos Chinquez, Juan de Quizman, Don Vasco de Procello, and Don Diago Vasquez, and these Captains: Espilando, Gallegardo, Maldamando, and Luis Fuentes. The Chronnicalor, Gonzado Quadrado Charmillo de Zafra who wrote (From the translations of B. F. French):

"We marched one day west from the Rio de Cannis in all this cold country this Wednesday, March 21, 1541, at the end of the day we came to a place called *Toalli*. All the Indians have houses built so, the houses are built of reeds in a manner of tules and daubed with mud which show as a mud wall, they are very clean and have a small door; when you shut it up and build a fire within it is as warm as in a stove."*

Don Luis De Moscoso and a scouting party traveled westward over the buffalo trail as far as the Trinity River before returning to the Adais.

For the next hundred and forty years this area was devoid of white explorers.

By early 1682 Cavalier Robert de LaSalle had begun descending the Mississippi River accompaneid by Henri De Tonty, the "Iron Hand", and a party of other Frenchmen.

April 9, 1682, LaSalle discovered the mouth of the Mississippi River and established a plaque there, claiming all land drained by this river for the King of France, Louis XIII. He named this land LOUISIANA in honor of King Louis and Queen Anna.

Returning up the Mississippi near a location in the Illinois country at Starving Rock in that same year he established Fort St. Louis and left Captain Henri De Tonty in command.

---

*The Red River near Natchitoches had an unusual cane growth and was later referred to as Rio Cannis by later Spaniards. The Adais lived on Spanish Lake as it was later called. This lake had an unusual heavy growth of cat-tails which resembled the Tules of Spain. *Toalli*, a slang, Spanish expression referring to houses built of tules. The mud and reed houses so described were typical of the Caddo Indian Federation of which the Adais was a tribe. The Caddo home or *Hinta-sak* was built so. The Adais were about a days march from the Red River-Natchitoches area, fifteen miles which was the usual distance foot soldiers traveled in that length of time.

LaSalle went to France and received assistance so that he could return and establish a settlement at the mouth of the Mississippi River. Through erroneous navigation the expedition missed the mouth of the Mississippi River and traveled westward, landing at Matagorda Bay, and in the Texas country established another Fort St. Louis in 1685.

LaSalle, realizing that this area was not suitable for colonization, began land excursions in an attempt to reach Canada.

Father Joutel's diary reveals that in January, 1687, he was with LaSalle, and a scouting party, were among the Nakassa Indians which resided on Nakassa Lake.*

In 1682 at Quaerataro, Mexico, The College of the Holy Cross was founded by Priests; Father Francois Hidalgo, Father Jose Diaz, Father Felix Isadore Espinosa, Father Nunez, Father Antonio de San Beunaventura Oliverez, Father Francisco Marino, Father Juan Parez, Father DeVaca, Father Salazar, Father Massinettes and Father Margil de Jesus, the last named, Father Margil de Jesus, being chosen as President of the College. These priests, so as to distinguish their work from the work of others called themselves *Zatachinies,* their purpose being to prepare others for frontier missionary duties. By 1684 they had succeeded in establishing missions south of the Rio Grande.

The most northern Spanish presidio at that time was Fort San Juan Bautista, located on the south bank of the Rio Grande near present day Eagle Pass, Texas. The land of the Coahuile Indians extended from present day San Antonio southward into the Monte Clova-Saltillo area of Mexico. The Matagordo area on the Gulf Coast was included in the land of the Coahuile.

Aside from the duties of the Spanish missions to spread the Catholic faith, they were also, in reality, observation and trading posts of the Spaniards. From one of these missions it was learned from an Indian who came to trade, that other white men had come out of the sea in large houses that floated on the waters of the gulf and had settled on the coast land.

On March 20, 1689, LaSalle was assassinated by some of his own men on a tributary of the Trinity River. Father Joutel

---

*Nakassa Lake is located in the southern part of Natchitoches Parish.

reported the men responsible for the assassination were in turn killed by the Indians. The remnants of the party returned to Fort St. Louis and finding it deserted, retraced their journey into the Trinity River area.

Alonzo DeLeon and Captain Flores were leading a scouting patrol when they found Santiago Grislet, Jean Lavaschevque and two very young boys, the Tulon brothers, Roberto and Pedro. This Spanish patrol searched for the next two months for other Frenchmen, but not being successful, returned to Mexico.

1689.

Juan Jarri had, during the absence of LaSalle, deserted Fort St. Louis and had risen to a lordly position among the tribes of the Coahuile Indians. During the search by DeLeon and Flores he had been shifted from tribe to tribe so that the Spanish Patrol failed to capture him. The Spanish now realized that this one Frenchman had the power to upset the semi-peacefulness of the Spanish frontier. The College of the Holy Cross was desiring to extend its Missionary work north of the Rio Grande.

Don Alonzo DeLeon, now the Spanish Governor of the Coahuile Territory, led an expedition to establish three missions among Hasinai Indians south of the Trinity River. He now also found himself in pursuit of a party of Frenchmen (Father Joutel's party).

Henri DeTonty at the Fort St. Louis near Starving Rock in the Illinois country, realized something was amiss and came in search of LaSalle. It is interesting to note how De Tonty, in all this vast country of the southern United Staes area chose the exact direction in which to travel. Probably the Caddo federation of Indians had trade agreements with the Indian tribes as far north as the Illinois and even further north among the Ouisconsins, to the west they traded with the Hasinais who in turn traded with the Coahuile Indians.

The Amole root (a species of the Yucca plant) was supplied to the Hasinais by the Coahuile Indians. The Caddos traded for this root, which had cleansing properties such as soap and when

Kinta-Sak A home of the Hopi Indians.

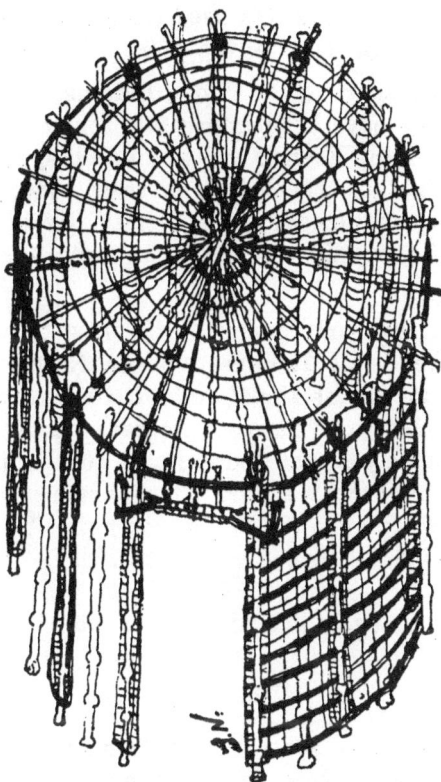

*Top view of hinta-sak show-
ing frame work and construction (Drawn by the author)*

ON OPPOSITE PAGE —

This drawing of a Caddo **hinta-sak,** or house, was made from the
description of an eye-witness, Gonzado Quadrado Charmillo, one of the
chroniclers of the De Soto expedition which visited the El Camino Real
area in 1540.

This Indian home was that of the Adais tribe near Robeline, La. of
the Caddo Federation. It was made of cypress poles and cane interlaced
with vines and daubed with a mixture of mud and moss. The roof was
covered with alligator skins which had been treated with bees-wax to make
it more impervious to rain. The broad leaves of the cat-tail plant were
inserted in the mud to prevent erosion from rain. Thus the Spanish
called the place **toai/le,** a deprecatory description of a house built of tules.
(Drawing by the author)

boiled in water this liquid was used for bathing purposes, it left a pleasant odor on the body of the user.

The Jumas, traders of the Caddo Indians, were also linguists and it would not have been impossible for them to distinguish the difference of the French and Spanish languages. The same Jumas of the Caddos traveled all of the Caddo trails. The Old Buffalo Trail extending from the Trinity River in Texas to the Red River in Louisiana was now considered part of the Caddo trail system.

In 1690 in the early spring De Tonty, "The Iron Hand," was among the Adais Indians and the Natchitoches Indians. He, too, went as far as the Trinity River in Texas, but there his guides refused to go further; he gave up his search for La-Salle. In the same year the Joutel Party found the Buffalo Trail beginning at the Trinity River. There among the Hasinai they learned of the Frenchman with the iron hand. They followed the Caddo trail and finally came in contact with De Tonty among the Arkansas Indians. Strangely enough, De Tonty actually came within one days march of finding the Joutel Party.

1690-1691

From the missions south to the Trinity River came the report of two French patrols in the vicinity of the Hainais which also coincided with the report of don Alonzo De Leon.

Late in 1690 the Don Domingo Teran Del Rios' expedition left Mexico, and scouted the complete area of the Caddo and Hasinai Federations of Indians; Teran listed the four tribes of the Hasinai as Bidia, Nabadache, Nadaco and the Nacogdoches. Of the Caddos were the Ais, the Adais, the Natchitoches, the Koasatas; he missed the Pedicaddo but listed the Caddoquopois near present day Fulton, Arkansas. He was the first white leader to sight Lake Bistineau. It is believed that the location Father Massinetes, who was with this expedition, established was La Mission Loretteto, near present day Ringgold, Louisiana.

For the reason Teran had not contacted any Frenchmen in all the territory and much to the disappointment of the members of the College of the Holy Cross, all missions north of the Rio Grande were withdrawn.

Padre Francois Hidalgo, being determined to establish missions north of the Rio Grande and among the Texas Indians, which were called by the Spaniards the Federation of Hasinai Indians, secured the support of the College of the Holy Cross to appeal to the Viceroy of Mexico. They only succeeded in obtaining permission to establish a mission at their own expense south of the Rio Grande but in an area visited by the Hasinai Indian traders. On November 7, 1698 Father Francois Hidalgo, assisted by Father Salazar, established the mission Maria de Los Delores, ten leagues north of Lampassas and ten leagues west of the Rio Sabinas. (Note: this Sabine River is not to be confused with the Sabine River which is the boundary between Louisiana and Texas).

From this outpost mission Francois Hidalgo conceived the idea of a "Chain of Missions" to extend to the very eastern edge of the Texas Indians' territory. He had at his disposal the reports of Father Massinetes and those of Teran and DeLeon. He knew that the land with its fertile soil and the enormous growth of forests, together with an abundance of wild game of the forests and fish of the lakes would supply many families of the frontier settlers with food and shelter. These families, who at this time were no better off than when they left Spain to settle in Mexico, would welcome such an opportunity.

1700

From the Journal of Father Paul De Ru. February 1, to May 8, 1700.

"Iberville, having founded the Fort at Biloxi, ascended the Mississippi River. At the village of the Tensas Iberville became ill but sent westward St. Denis and Bienville with nineteen other Frenchmen, two of whom were the Tulon brothers, Roberto and Piedro;* at the village of the Tensas was a Wichita Indian whose

---

*These were the same two brothers which were captured by DeLeon and Flores, and been put on a Spanish ship to be returned to France. The ship was captured by the French and these two were with Iberville when he landed at Biloxi.

tribe had settled near the Tensas." This Indian declared he had visited a Spanish mission in the Texas Country (The mission Maria de Los Delores). The Indian was immediately employed by Bienville as a guide.

On April 20, 1700 the St. Denis-Bienville party reached the Yatasee village on Nantanchie Lake near present day Montgomery, Louisiana (See Location 5 on map).

The Frenchmen were among the Natchitoches Indians (Location 8 on map), on May 8, 1700 for on this day Bienville departed with Father Paul De Ru leaving St. Denis to scout the locations of the Caddo Indians. Bienville, having secured pirogues from the Natchitoches Indians, returned by water down the Red River to the Mississippi and back to Biloxi. St. Denis soon followed and brought with him a number of the Natchitoches Tribe of Indians, who settled on the north shore of Lake Pontchartrain. St. Denis settled near by at Fort Louis.

1701-1707

During these years Father Hidalgo and Father Salazar were trading and preaching to the Indians at Mission Maria de Los Delores. Father Hidalgo traded with the Indians for gold; Anya, who was then the Governor of Coahuile, was aware of this. There are several historical records referring to the raiding of the Hidalgo mission in search of gold. Hidalgo at first did turn the gold over to the government, part of which was to be given to the College of the Holy Cross. A Captain Hernandez was broken in rank when he gave Hidalgo a receipt for the gold. Padre Hidalgo realized that very little, if any, of the gold was reaching the King of Spain.

Anya conceived the idea of cutting off the supplies of trade goods to the mission so that the Indians would then have to come and trade at the Presidio San Juan Bautista. Captain Hernandez upon the urgence of the Priests of the College was restored to rank. Father Hidalgo, realizing that no one would actually know how much gold he was accumulating, began to hoard the gold.

1708

Allarge Bejoux, operating from a location near present day Pointe Coupee, had cut a road or trail overland northwestward to intersect the Buffalo Trail west of the present town of Many, Louisiana, and had by the year 1708 established trade agreements for horses with the Ais Indians (See location 10 on map). Francois Hidalgo through his trade with the Indians of different tribes soon learned of this.

A Legend of the Flores Family

Hidalgo and Salazar with assistance had solicited the aid of the Flores families of Saltillo, some of whom were merchants and others owners of landed estates. The merchants supplied the mission de Los Delores with trade supplies.

Through Bernardino, Sub-chief of the Hasinai Indians, Hidalgo learned of a meeting place called Campti, where each Fall of every year all of the tribes of the Caddo Federation of Indians gathered for sports and trading purposes. (Campti was the name of the Chief of the Natchitoches tribe who had organized this meeting, held on a great sand-bar near present-day Campti, Louisiana). These meetings were of a secret nature and not sanctioned by the Spanish Government, and the tradition of their occurrence had remained with the Flores family. Hidalgo prevailed on the Flores family, who knew the value of land and what it could produce for settlers, to assist him by sending men to go on a trading expedition to the Campti. Bernardino was to act as guide.

Ramone Flores and a cousin, Joseph Colliea, were designated by the elder Flores to go and assist the Spanish priests. These two made four trips in the Fall of the years 1708, 1709, 1710 and 1711 to the Sand-bar near *Campti, Louisiana.*

The Letter

Francois Hidalgo committed an action which might well be considered treason by the Spanish Government. He wrote three letters of the same content, all dated January 17, 1711, addressed to the Governor of Louisiana. Only one reached its destination. In mid-summer of 1713 the Governor of Louisiana, La Mothe de Cadillac, had the letter in his possession. (There is always an incident in history which incites a chain reaction in such a way that a new era begins, always resulting in the establishment of new frontiers. The Hidalgo letter was such an incident).

One must surmise how such a letter could travel through nearly a thousand miles of wilderness and reach its destination. The whole new frontier of El Camino Real hinged on this accomplishment.

The contents of the letter showed that Father Hidalgo had first-hand knowledge of the land of the Hasinai and the Caddos as well as the waterways of the adjoining area. He wrote that the French traders were to ascend the Mississippi to the confluence of the Red River, then ascend the Red River to the tribe of the Natchitoches Indians, thence to travel westward over the Buffalo Trail to the Hasinai Indians and there procure guides to the Hidalgo Mission.

Father Hidalgo could have acquired knowledge of the Caddo area from the reports of De Leon, Teran and Father Massinetes but he would have not had the knowledge of the waterways, which could have only been obtained from the Natchitoches Indians who may have come to the Campti from their location on the north shore of Lake Pontchartrain; information was given to Flores and Colliea and passed on to Hidalgo.

The letter was an invitation "to come and trade" with the Hidalgo mission, the word "trade" being used as bait could have come from two sources, that of Bejoux to the Ais and that of Flores and Colliea. It is possible that Hidalgo wrote the letters very early in the year so that one could be sent to the Ais Tribe ahead of the arrival of Allarge Bejoux. The later two letters were carried in the Fall of the year by Flores and Colliea, who in turn gave the letters directly to a Natchitoches Indian who had come to the Campti, but who was living on the north shore of Lake Pontchartain. Several historians say that St. Denis had the letter in his possession before it was presented to Governor Cadillac. St. Denis through his association with the Natchitoches

Indians, who were settled near his Fort Louis, would have been the most logical Frenchman to receive the letter. Then, too, St. Denis, while vying with Cadillac to be sent as the leader on the trading expedition to the Hidalgo mission, had stated that he and Jules Lambert, who was at that time in the Illinois country, had been on a trading trip to the Natchitoches Indians in the summers of 1710 and 1712. Here, then, is another possbility that St. Denis may have received the first letter sent by Francois Hidalgo by an Indian messenger to the Ais, and who was instructed to give the letter to the first Frenchman who came to trade in his area.

The letter had the desired effect; St. Denis was appointed to lead the expedition. Cadillac chose wisely because St. Denis was an educated man, and was a third generation Canadian and, further, he understood the ways of the Indians. He was a linguist and could speak many Indian dialects, and also speak, read and write in Spanish.

The trading expedition, consisting of Indians of the Natchitoches tribe, left Biloxi in mid October, 1713. Among the Indians were the White Chief, his son, Koanan, and two daughters, one called *Quilchil*, "the pretty weaver," and the other called *Olchogonime*, "the good girl."

The Jean Penicaut narrative is an actual eye witness account of St. Denis' journey to Natchitoches and on to Mexico. The party consisted of nearly forty Indians and twenty-three Frenchmen, two of whom were St. Denis and Penicaut, and several French traders, Pierre Largen, Jean Lagross, Roberto Talon, Pedro Talon, Lafrinaries, Allarge Bejoux, Labinaries, Enrique Lantillac; Medar Jalot, who was valet and doctor to St. Denis; the two Barberousse brothers were hunters for the party's food; *Rambin* was a tailor. Soldiers in the party included Lt. Phillippe Blondell, De Lery, De Muy, Williard Anvillaries, De Beaulieux, De Voixant, Frainbouis, and Lavasseur, who was also a map maker.

Leaving Biloxi, the party traveled what was then known as the Iberville pasage, crossing Lake Pontchartrain and through Manchac Pass to Lake Maurepas, then into Manchac Bayou and a short portage to the Mississippi River; ascending the Mississippi to the confluence of the Red River at Baton Rouge, then ascending the Red River to a point opposite the present day town of Colfax. Here the stream divided and Penicaut wrote, "we took the left and larger branch of water." After some distance upstream he describes the Ecore de La Croix, which must have been the high bluffs near Chopin, Louisiana.

On November 25, 1713, the St. Denis party arrived among the Natchitoches Indians, living on an island that the river formed by dividing into two branches and flowing around it.

St. Denis spent the first few weeks cultivating the friendship of the Indians. Trade was vigorous and profitable, he sent at least twice back to Biloxi for more trade goods. He had traveled at least once as far as the settlement of the Nacogdoches Indians before deciding on an exact location for a trading post. In early Spring of the following year two block houses were erected in the Natchitoches Village, one to store the merchandise and the other to house the ten Frenchmen who were to remain in Natchitoches while the others went west in search of the Hidalgo mission.

While St. Denis was among the Hasinai Indians, an incident happened which causes one to wonder at the foresightedness of Francois Hidalgo. Among the Indians was an Indian maid named Angelica who had received instructions at a Spanish mission and who spoke Spanish fluently. She became the interpreter between St. Denis and Bernardino, Chief of the Hasinai. Bernardino, with some of the members of his tribe, acted as guide, for St. Denis, but instead of bringing the Frenchmen to the Hidalgo mission, they were led to Presidio San Juan Bautista on the south bank of the Rio Grande River on July 19, 1714. Surely these Indians would have known where the Hidalgo mis-

---

PLAN OF FORT NATCHITOCHES—opposite page

A.	Church.	E.	Barracks of the militia.
B.	Home of the Commandante.	F.	Guardhouse.
C.	Gunpowder and arm storage.	G.	Dining hall for soldiers.
D.	House of the priest, and where records were kept.	H.	Houses of domestic servants and kitchen.
		I.	Privy.

PLAN DU FORT DES NATCHITOCHE

A. l'église construite de poteaux en terre enduite en
pierre, bouzillé entre les joints et couverte d'aores

B. Maison du command. bouzillé aussi de la terre

C. Poudriere de mesme construction

D. Magazin fait a la fin de 1732 de mesme construction que l'église

E. caserne de mesme construction construite a la
fin de 1732

F. Corps de garde de mesme construction

G. Logement du garde magazin de mesme construction

H. Mauvaise baraques qui servent de cuisine
et à logeu les domestiques et negres

I. four pour le pain

N.a. que toute l'enceinte du fort n'est que ce gros pieux
de neuf pieds d'hauteur hors de terre, redouble en dedans avec
deux de six dans pieds hors de pur

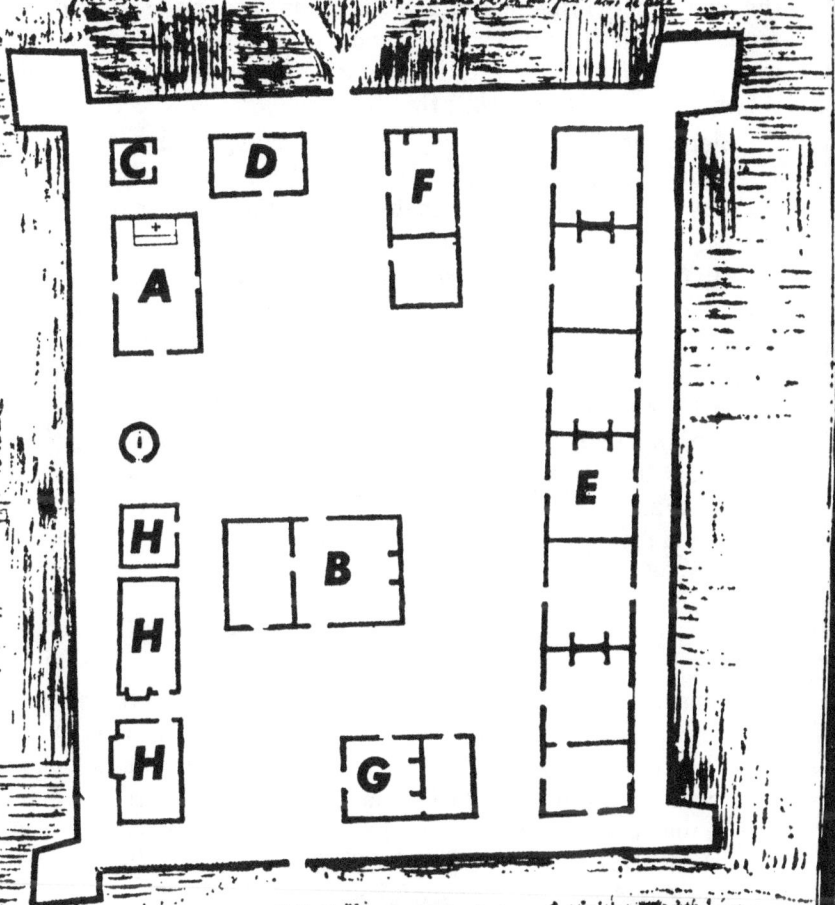

Riviere Rouge

a la nouvelle orleans
ce 15 janvier 1733

sion was located; the leading of the Frenchmen to the Spanish post was just as Hidalgo would have wished, or planned.

There was quite an uproar at Post Du Nord, as the French called the Presidio San Juan Bautista. The French trade-goods were confiscated, and St. Denis was confined to the area inside the presidio. Somehow St. Denis found out about the plans of the Spansih priests to establish missions to the east, and sent word back to Bienville. The Frenchman knew that very often presidios followed the establishments of missions. Bienville was informed by St. Denis that this land belonged to the French.

Claud De Tisne was dispatched to Natchitoches to build a Fort in 1716, Post St. Jean Baptista Des Natchitoches, naming the post after the title given by St. Denis when the two block houses were built in the spring of 1714.

St. Denis remained in the custody of the Spanish from 1714 until February 17, 1716, when he arrived at Presidio San Juan Bautista. When the Don Domingo Ramone expedition left Saltillo, Mexico, St. Denis was selected as guide, along with several other Frenchmen, Medar Jalot, the two Talon brothers, Pierre Largen and Jean Lagross. The other Frenchmen who were with St. Denis had previously returned to Natchitoches, undoubtedly carrying messages for St. Denis. Medar Jalot declared later that he had delivered messages four times for St. Denis, thus the French had been kept well informed of the goings-on of the Spanish.

St. Denis while on this adventure married a Spanish wife, Manuella Sanchez Ramone, daughter of the Alverez, Don Diego Ramone at the Spanish Presidio. He left her at the presidio, which was also her home, and returned to Natchitoches.

The Ramone expedition established the following Missions: San Francisco de Los Delores on the Neches River, La Purisima Conception on the Angelina River, Mission San Jose, North of Nacogdoches, and Mission Neustra Senora de Guadelupe at Nacogdoches.
All of these were established in 1716.

In 1717 father Margil de Jesus and Father Francois Hidalgo established two missions further to the east, La Mission Nuestra

LA PRESIDIO NUESTRA SENORA DE LOS DELORES

La Presidio Nuestra Senora de Los Delores was erected by Domingo Ramone in the summer of 1716. It was later repaired by the Marquis De Aguayo in 1722. The plan of the fort is the work of Aguayo. The fort overlooked Los Torres, or Mill Creek, near the intersection of the lower Douglas Road and the road from Douglas to Wells just west of Nacogdoches, Texas. This presidio was erected and garrisoned to protect the three Missions in the near Nacogdoches vicinity.

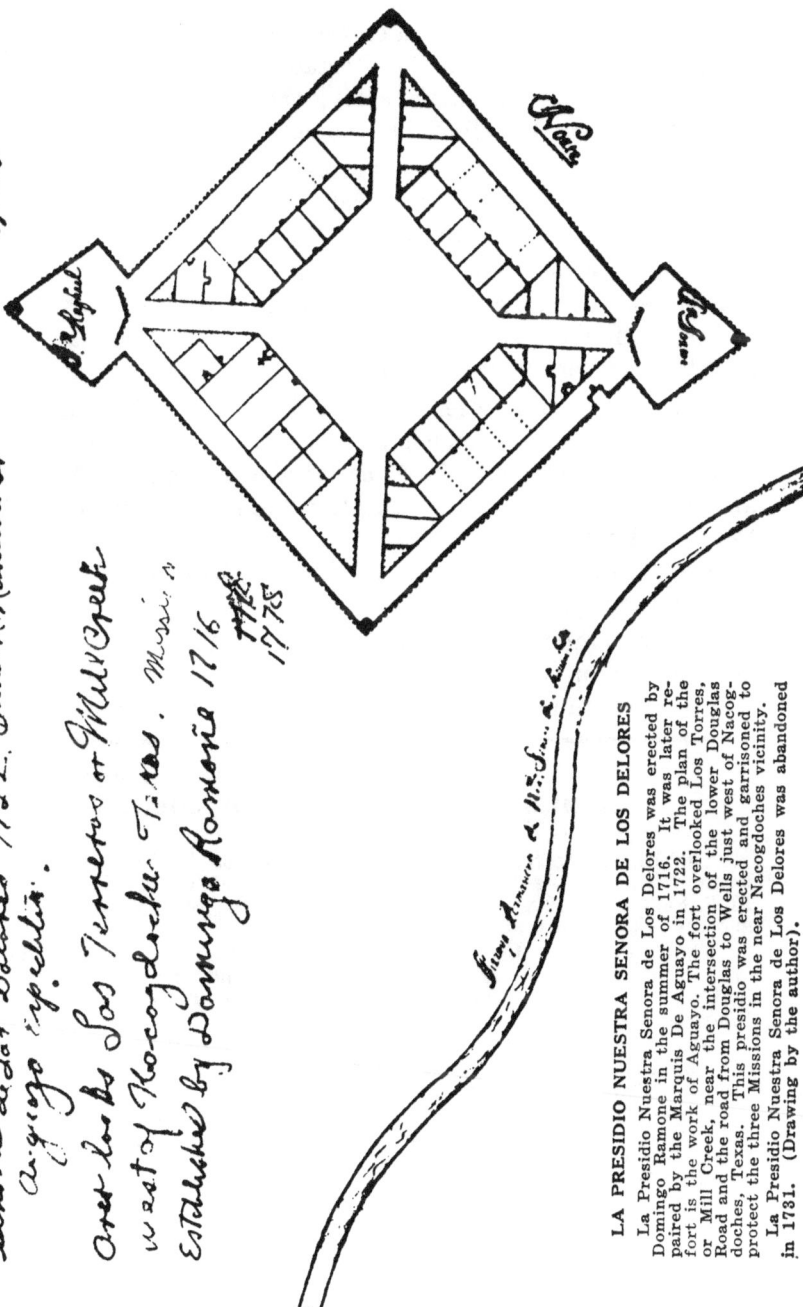

La Presidio Nuestra Senora de Los Delores was abandoned in 1781. (Drawing by the author).

de Los Delores among the Ais Indians, near the present day city of San Augustine, Texas, and on the first day of St. Michael the Archangel, September 29, 1717 established La Mission de San Miguel Cuellar de Los Adais, among the Adais Indians, one mile north of present Robeline, Louisiana.

At this moment Father Francois Hidalgo's vision had come into being—after twenty-five years of dreaming, he had established his chain of missions to the very end of the Texas Country.

With the establishment of this last mission among the Adais Indians just fifteen miles away from the French post at Natchitoches, both the French and Spanish realized that each must maintain settlements so as to hold the territories thus far gained.

War broke out between France and Spain in 1719 and in that same year Phillipe Blondell from the French post among the Natchitoches Indians, raided the mission among the Adais and allowed one prisoner to escape after making known to him that the French were coming in multitudes to drive the Spanish back. This caused a withdrawal of all Spanish Missions in the Texas area as far as San Antonio.

Every country has its "man of the minute", and this country of New Spain was no exception. He offered his wealth and abilities to restore the Texas missions and to re-occupy the Texas

---

OPPOSITE PAGE
LA MISSION DE SAN MIGUEL DE CUELLAR
DE LOS ADAIS

The Mission de San Miguel de Cuellar de Los Adais was founded by Padre Margil de Jesus and Padre Francois Hidalgo on September 29, 1717. September 29 was also the Feast Day of St. Michael the Arch Angel and the Mission was named for him.

The site of this Mission is one-half mile northwest of Robeline, Louisiana, on a hill which overlooks a small valley, and across the valley one-half mile north of another hill was the Presidio de Nuestra Senora del Pilar de Los Adais.

Fra Jose de Solice visited the Adais area in 1767 and kept a Diary of his visitation in which he noted that the Mission Records showed: 256 Baptisms, 64 Marriages and 116 Burials.

In this Diary were listed the names of families he visited in the Adais area: Bano, Cachon, Flores, Bustamenta, Garcia, Solice, Martinez, Sanchez, Rodriguez, Sanchon, Mora, Benetis, Cartinez, Carlos, Vega and La Lima, y Barbo, Cazorla, Fuente, Gallerado and Gonzalez. Cardova, Duro, Mancheca, Solice, Mercado, Guerra, and Bautimino.

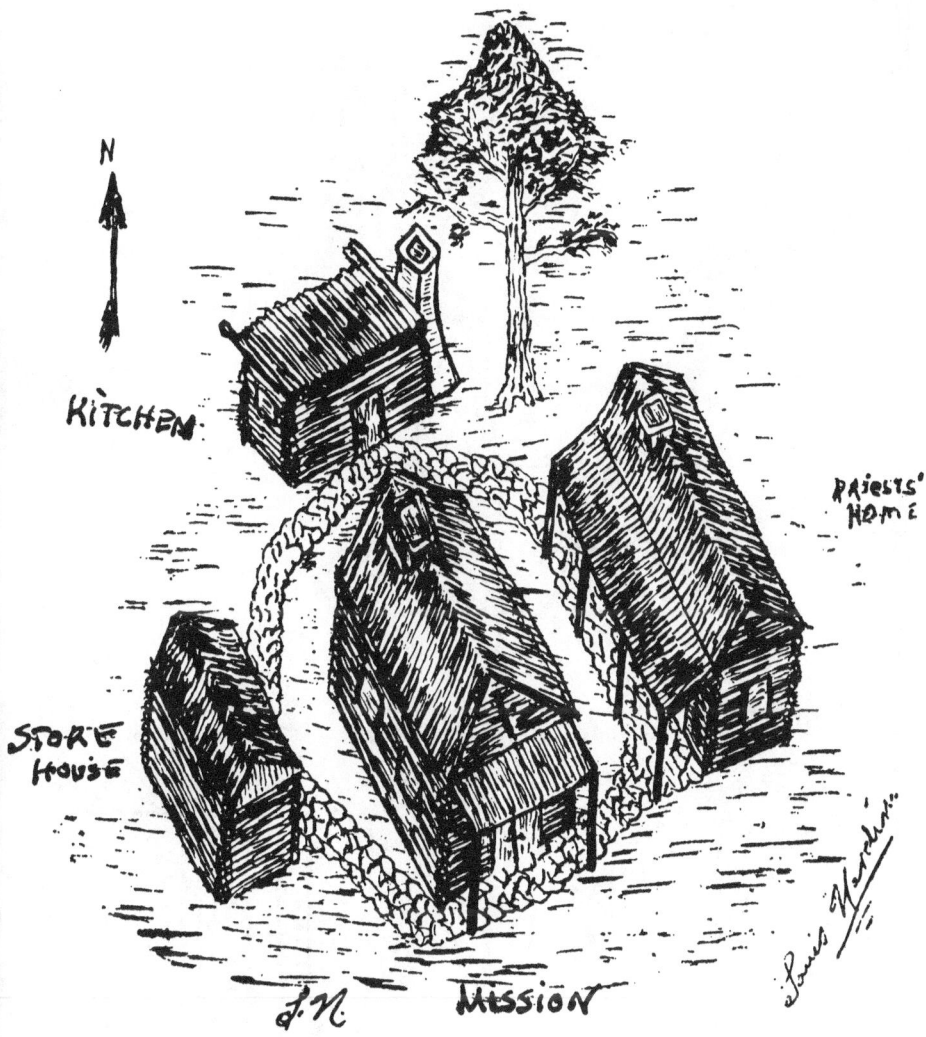

N

KITCHEN

PRIESTS' HOME

STORE HOUSE

J.N. MISSION

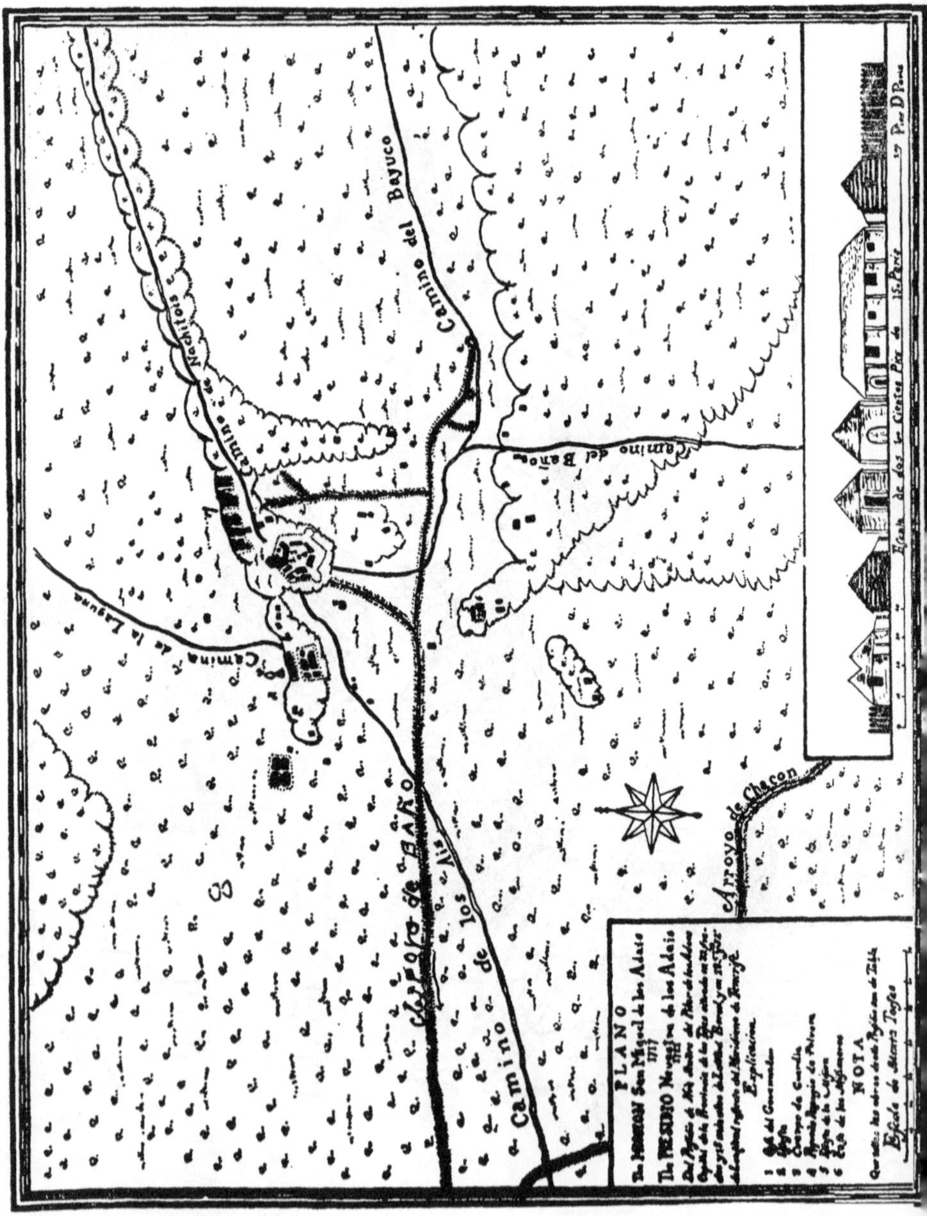
Camino de Nachitois
Camino del Bayuco
Camino del Baños
Camino de la Laguna
Arroyo de Baño
Camino de los Ais
Arroyo de Chacon

OPPOSITE PAGE —

Explanation of map of: La Mission San Miguel de Cuellar de Los Adais and Mission established September 29, 1717; Del Presidido de Neustra Senora del Pilar de Los Adais, presidio established November 1721.

PLAN. This presidio shown on this map of 1722 was the Capitol of the Providence of Texas and is located at 32 degrees and 15 minutes latitude and 285 degrees and 52 minutes longitude. The scale, Toise, one Toise equals six feet. The present day location is one mile north of Robeline, Louisiana, just one quarter mile west of Highway Six from that point.

Camino del Bayuco, road to Bayuco. (Bayuco, a house of Entertainment— A Night Club of that period.)

Camino de los Ais, road to the Ais tribe of Indians at San Augustine, Texas. This was the dry weather trail and passed through Marthaville, Belmont, Zwolle and Ebarb, Louisiana.

Camino de la Laguna, road to swampy lake area, Spanish Lake.

Camino del Bano, road to Rancho aBno, allotted to the Mission, also a part of El Camino Real.

Arroyo de Chacon, small river of Chacon, named after Chacon who had settled on the Creek—Winn Break today.

(Chacon is also a Spanish dance which had its own music set to special tempo.)

---

country. The new governor of Coahuile and the Texas region was the Marquis de San Miguel de Aguayo, his title was Don Joseph de Alzar, Knight Commandante de Aragon, Governor and Captain General of the Provinces of Texas-New Phillippines and of Coahuile, New Kingdom of Estrandura—and he had earned every one.

By the middle of October, 1720, the Aguayo expedition was well on its way to the Los Adais area, with three thousand nine hundred fifty horses and six hundred mules, loaded with powder, shot, food, clothing and six cannons, five hundred eighty-four men *AND* two hundred thousand piastres to build presidios on the frontier.

Aguayo, while en-route to Los Adais, received word the war between France and Spain had ended and there would be no war on the frontier, never the less, Aguayo established the missions and the Presidio San Antonio de Bexar at San Antonio. At the tribe of the Adais he began proceedings to establish a presidio there. France, too, had their "man of the minute" in the person of St. Denis.

With St. Denis came the balance of power, which is necessary on any frontier. The Spanish had the French out-numbered ten

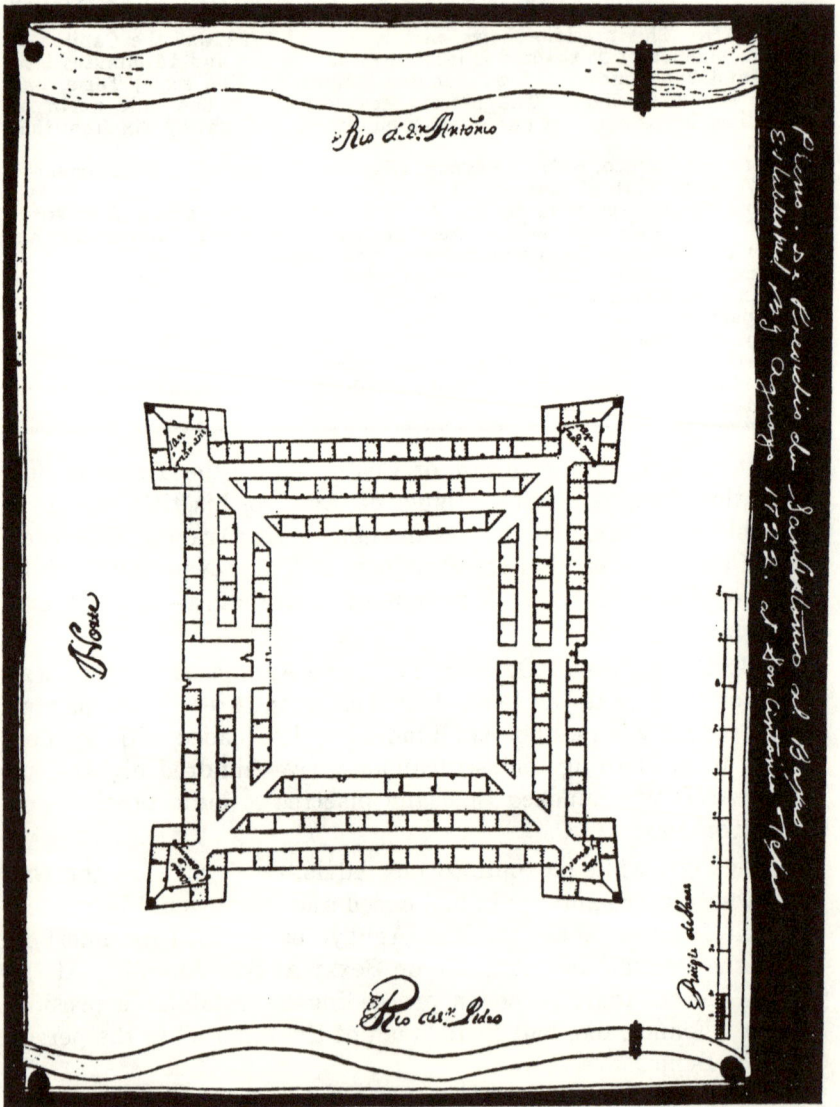

Plano de Presidio de Sandiclario d'Bejar
establecido a 3 de Agosto 1722, a Don Antonio Tello

Rio d'San Antonio

Norte

Rio de San Pedro

Piesis d'altura

OPPOSITE PAGE
LA PRESIDIO DE SAN ANTONIO DE BEXAR

La Presidio de San Antonio de Bexar, established by Aguayo in 1722, was located at San Antonio, Texas.

The work of Aguayo in establishing the presidios along El Camino Real gave permanence and protection to the Spanish settlers who were to follow, from San Antonio to the Adais in Louisiana, seeking a new kind of freedom. Their source of food and other essentials was so far away that they learned to live "off the land", and became dependent on no one. As far as they were concerned the head of the Spanish Government was so far away he was only a figure of speech to them. This freedom was bred into their descendants — the seed cast by Francois Hidalgo, fortified by Aguayo, nourished by El Camino Real and the Neutral Strip was to blossom into the State of Texas at San Antonio.

NEXT PAGE
PLAN OF FT. DEL PILAR DE LOS ADAIS

1. House of the Governor.
2. Church, which w a s enclosed within the Presidio.
3. Houses of the Soldier's stationed there.
4. Powder Magazine.
5. La Mission San Miguel de Cuellar de Los Adais.
6. Priests' home.
7. Dwellings of the Adais Tribe of Indians.
8. The Rancho of La Lima, possibly the first merchant and Indian trader of the Spanish in this area.

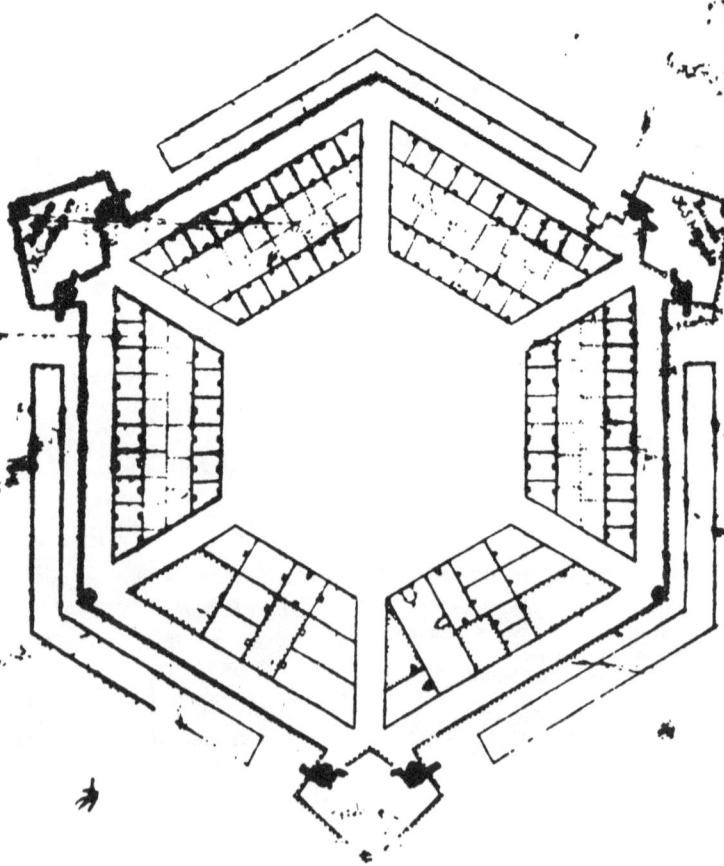

Arroyo permanente todo el año

to one, but they also knew that the tribes of the Caddo Federation favored St. Denis and the French. The gold piasters were of special attraction, as they would have been in any locality, to St. Denis, who was an accomplished trader. Aguayo was quick to realize that the Spanish must trade with the French for food and their very existence. He turned a deaf ear to Captain Reynaud, St. Denis and Bienville, who was now the Governor of Louisiana, and their protests concerning the building of a presidio at Los Adais, and on October 12, 1721 celebrated the rebuilding of the mission. On November 1st in the same year was celebrated the re-establishment of La Presidio de Nuestra Senora del Pilar de Los Adais—the Presidio housing the Governor of all the province of Texas.

In 1722 St. Denis was made Post Commandante of Fort St. Jean Baptiste des Natchitoches and all of the Red River Territory.

Breutin's map of 1722 of the Natchitoches area, shows the names of inhabitants who owned land: Durion, Derbonne, Duplisses, Marachal, Lebrun, Boquet, Prudhomme, LaFleur, Roland, St. Denis, Dauphine, Rondain, Frainbouis, Rambin, Robert and Frainaries.

Other known inhabitants of the Natchitoches area were: Redot, Lieutenant of the Company of the West; Marley Dupuy, Ensigne; Medar Jalot, St. Denis' valet; Pierre Cotolleau, farmer; Pierre Fausse, Farmer; Francois Berry, soldier; Francois Lemoine, soldier; Estinne LeRoy, soldier; Pierre DuBois, blacksmith; Marainne Benoist, housewife; Louise Francois Gillot, housewife; Pierre Dupuy, called Gaupillion, to distinguish him from Dupuy the ensigne; Jeanne Grinot, housewife; Collette de Poissot, housewife; Marie Cathern de Poutree, housewife; Martine Bonnet, housewife; Antoniette Audebrands, housewife; Pierre Marineau; Sieur De Champingnole, sergeant; Lieutenant Maillard; Louis Reclos, soldier; Emanuella Sanchez Ramone, wife of St. Denis; Sieur Barme, storekeeper; and Jean Lagross and the two Barberousse brothers who had settled near Campti, establishing a trading post among the Yatasee Indians, which had moved from Nantanchie Lake in 1722.

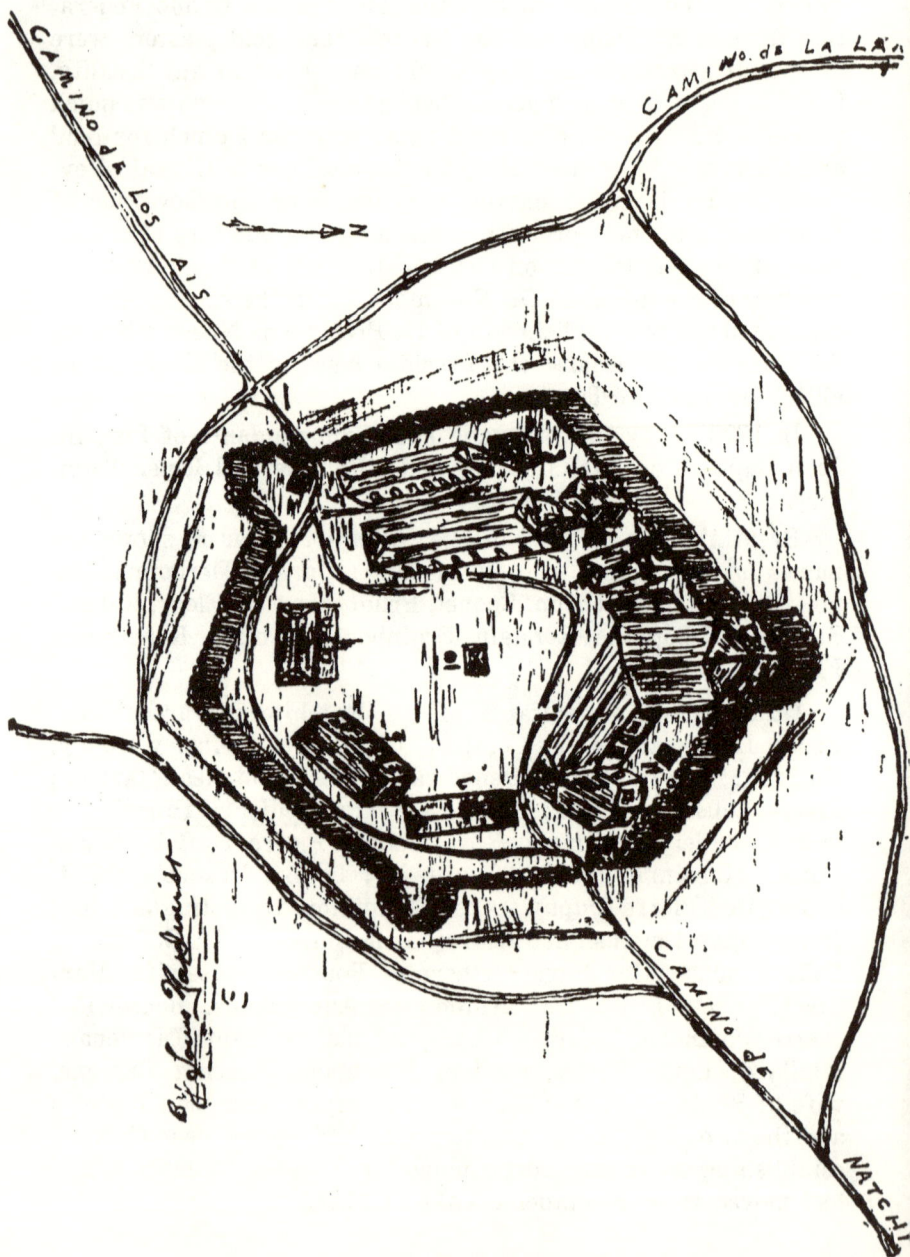

LA PRESIDIO NUESTRA DE SENORA DEL PILAR
DE LOS ADAIS

Established in November 1721 and completed early in the Spring of 1722 by the Marquis de Aguayo.

Knights in Armour are usually associated with the European countries and the valiant deeds accomplished by such men, but here on this tiny hill among the Adais Indians two Knights met, The Marquis de Aguayo, a Black Knight of the Argonne, and Louis Juchereau de St. Denis, who had previously received The Order of the Cross of St. Louis delivered to St. Denis by D'Artagnan, a direct envoy of the King and Queen of France. Thus, two Knights met at the Adais, supped and visited, each recognized the abilities of the other, each having received the highest honor which could be bestowed by their respective King.

1.	Governor's House.	6.	Mess Hall.
2.	Church.	7.	Kitchen.
3.	Soldier's Barracks.	8.	Privy.
4.	Guardhouse.	9.	Powder Magazine.
5.	Stables.	10 and 11.	Water wells.

This Spanish Fort was erected in the shade of a hexagon. Aguayo had six cannons and building the Fort in this shape permitted the greatest amount of cannon fire in all directions. One will notice that on the hilltop, the site of this Spanish presidio, several hundred yards in all directions there is an absence of large tress and that those that are growing are second and third-growth trees. The reason is that Aguayo followed the same methods a trained military officer would have done. He would have cleared the Land of all trees and undergrowth for at least three hundred yards in all directions, so that should an attack occur, the enemy would not have the benefit of any kind of natural cover. The shoulder guns of that period had a fairly accurate killing effect for a distance of 150 yards. Therefore the Musketeer in the presidido would have some extra 150 yards in which to sight the enemy, take aim and fire. This presidio is unique in this respect: It stood for nearly fifty years as a frontier command-post and never once had to defend itself.

This plan of the Presidio at Los Adais, showing the effectiveness of a hexagon shaped fort with cannon spaced to give the maximum protection to the fort, was submitted to Aguayo to his superiors at Mexico City in 1722.

The Presidio Nuestra Senora del Pilar de Los Adais has a very unique history, it stood guarding a frontier against another nation and among the Indians, who were at that time, considered savages, for nearly fifty years, yet this fort never had to defend itself against any hostile demonstration.

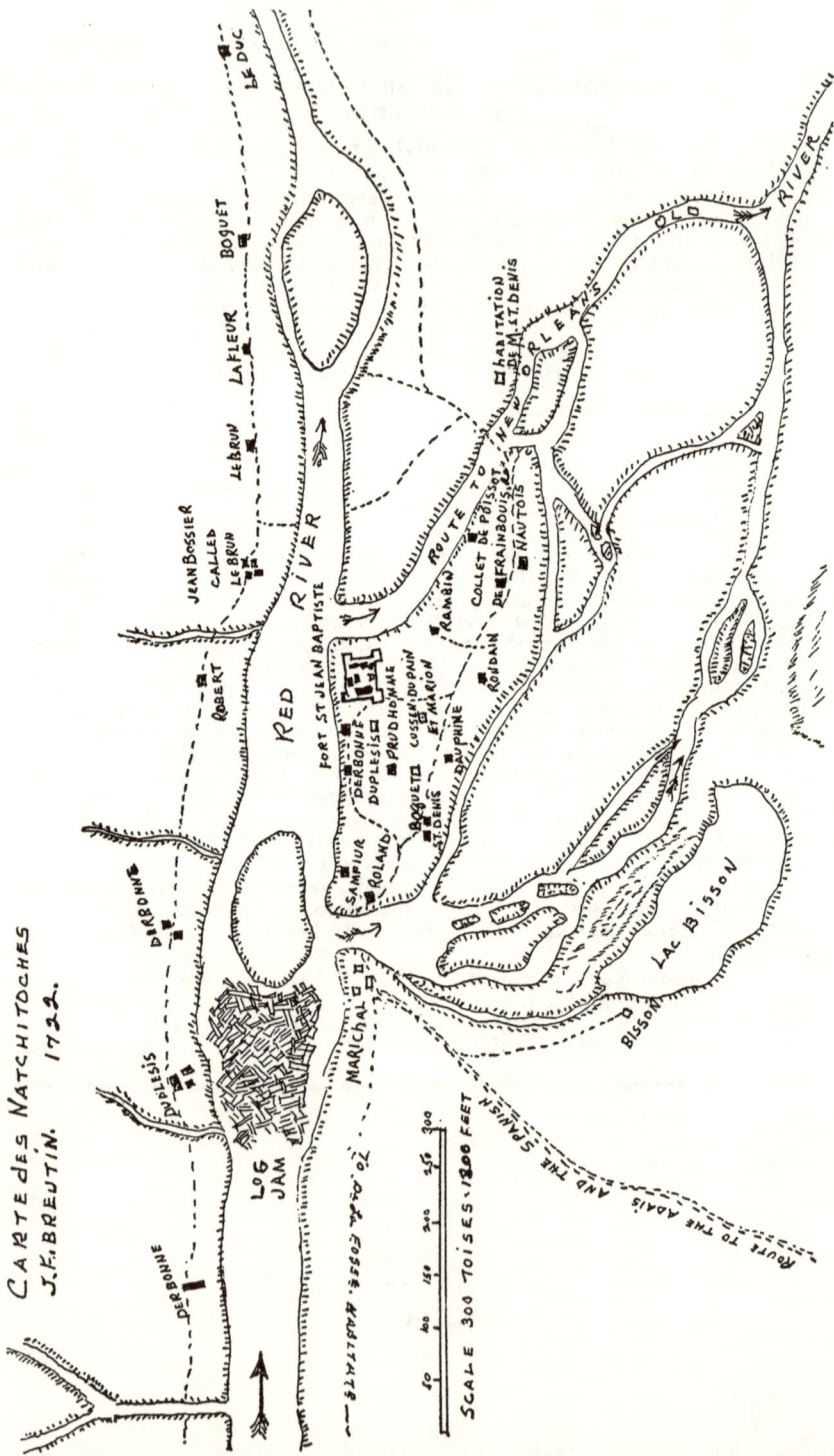

CARTE DES NATCHITOCHES
J.F. BREUTIN. 1722.

RED RIVER

OLD RIVER

RIVER

NEW ORLEANS

LE DUC
BOGUET
LAFLEUR
LE BRUN
CALLED
LE BRUN
JEAN BOSSIER
ROBERT

HABITATION
DE M. T. DENIS
COLLET DE POISSON
FRAINBOURG
NAUTOIS
RAMBIN
RONDAIN

FORT ST JEAN BAPTISTE
DERBONNE
PRUDHOMME
DUPLESIS
COSSE DU PAIN
ET MARION
BOQUET
ST DENIS
DAUPHINE
SAMPIUR
ROLAND

DERBONNE

DUPLESIS

DERBONNE

LOG JAM
MARICHAL

LAC BISSON
BISSON

ROUTE TO POISSON

ROUTE TO THE ADAIS AND THE SPANISH

TO TOISE 300 FEET FROM NATCHITOCHES

SCALE 300 TOISES = 1800 FEET

30   60   150   300   450   600

Pierre Largen was trading among the Peticaddos and the Caddoquopois.

La Petit was among the Peticaddos on Caddo Lake near Shreveport, he had the year previously established a trading post there.

Jean Lagross, who had also married an Ais maiden, had a trading post among the Ais Indians on the Angelena River near the present town of San Augustine, Texas. He was not molested by the Spanish because of the marriage he was considered a member of the Caddos of which the Ais was a tribe.

In 1723 St. Denis sent Lieutenant Antoine Layassard to establish Post Du Rapides near present Alexandria. The year previously LaPerrier and his two daughters had been assassinated at the rapids portage by a band of roving Indians, and Post Du Rapides was established to protect travelers en-route to Post des Natchitoches.

In this same year, 1723 St. Denis received reinforcements, Doctor Alexander, Lt. Basset, Lt. Renault de Hautrive and Paul Muller. Michael Robin, a Notary for the Company of the West was also in the group.

Augayo, tiring of the frontier, left for the interior of Mexico. He appointed as Lieutenant Governor of Los Adais, Lieutenant of the King, Almazon, who immediately set up a new trade restriction, forbidding fraternalization and trading of any sort with the French. It was during the tenure of Almazon that a land grant was issued to Juan Sanchez comprising one square league of land (the grant was an area now consisting of high ground astraddle Toplecot Creek in the Allen area between Robeline and Powhattan, Louisiana). Almazon allotted land to Cadet Chacon. There was also land allotted for the support of the Adais mission called Rancho Bano. Manuel Guiterez, who had wed Maria Garcia, also received an allotted land grant. The last three allotments of land were in the immediate Robeline township area.

St. Denis could see permanence in this establishment of farms in the Adais area. The presidio there now had a fighting force of one hundred men-at-arms, many of which were well-mounted and excellent cavalry men. He could to a certain extent visualize a self supporting Spanish frontier if the farmers' production of crops were successful. The Spanish would need only slight assistance from the Indian farmers with the sale of their produce to the Spanish.

St. Denis retaliated by inviting all of the chiefs of the Caddo tribes of Indians to come to the Post St. Jean Baptiste to receive presents, knowing that all of the chiefs would bring their families and a number of followers and that many would have to pass the Spanish presidios on their way to Natchitoches. He was successful in working out a trade agreement with all of the tribes to buy their entire surplus food supply.

This alliance of the Caddo federation with the French restored the balance of power on the Spanish-French frontier. St. Denis assured the Caddo chiefs that each year such presents would be available as long as the alliance was kept.

This one move by St. Denis brought safety to the French of the area. Thus any unpleasantness which arose thereafter was confined to verbal statements or letter writing.

III

DACHICOIN — A NOBLE INDIAN
LOS ADAIS, 1723

Dachicoin had only two years before he reached the considered age of an adult, which according to the Adais law was sixteen. He had ignited the council-fire of the Adais and was demanding audience. The Elders came and seated themselves in their proper places and bade his speak.

He brought to the attention of the Adais how nice the Spanish or French treated an Indian of position in any Indian tribe— they dared not molest this Indian or any of his family. Also, the Indian of position seemed to get a better deal in the matter of trade-goods. "If we make all the Indian adult males of the Adais an officer or man of position then the whole tribe will benefit by it. I wish first to test this and, if I am successful, then I demand to be made a *conachas*".* Dachicoin explained

Dachicoin went to the Natchitoches Post and demanded of Sieur Barme, a merchant of certain trade-goods, a supply of such goods, saying that he would bring all the profit back to the merchant in return for which he expected something that he could trade for himself at profit. Sieur Barme saw possibilities in Dachicoin because he agreed to the Indian's terms. Sieur Barme did not overlook the fact that the Indian spoke to him in French. Later he found out that the Indian also spoke Spanish. Dachicoin was made a *conachas* among the Adais. his proposed test to the Elders.

---
*An official of rank next only to the chief.

When Dachicoin was fifteen years old the Spanish priests came to the Adais. Even at this young age he must have realized that a new way of life was beginning among the Adais, and decided to follow the new trend by working with the Spanish priests, guiding them among the tribes of the Caddos and commuting back and forth with them to the Natchitoches post. Soon he mastered the Spanish language. When he was sixteen and had successfully filled the agreement of his first test with Sieur Barme, the Natchitoches merchant, three other men, Lotbotiniere, Lagross and Largen, saw the possibility of profit in the use of Dachicoin. One or the other of these traders was continuously traveling back and forth to the Hasinai Indians who lived deep in the Tejas Country. So Dachicoin began a tutorship with the traders, and at the same time began to master the French language.

In 1719 Dachicoin, because he could understand French, heard of the salt shortage at the new post at New Orleans. By this time the young Indian trader had acquired five horses as his part of profit while trading with the Hasinai Indians. He went to Sieur Barme and asked for ten knives, explaining that he wished to trade the knives to the Destonies for salt, this salt would be taken to New Orleans and traded for more knives which would be returned to Sieur Barme. He would replace the ten knives and the other remaining knives would be divided equally between himself and the merchant. He would leave two horses with Sieur Barme as security. Dachicoin then went to Largent, who had dug-out canoes. He wished use of the largest one, explaining his intention to Largen, and leaving one of his horses with him as security. In return for the use of the canoe Dachicoin would take some of Largen's merchandise of furs to New Orleans and trade the furs for knives, all Largen needed to do was to say how many knives he expected in trade for the furs—of course this service would be free for the use of the boat. The Indian then went to Lieutenant Blondell, the Post Commandante, and told him his intentions, wondering if the officer had letters he wished to be delivered to his French superiors, saying that he would deliver the letters which at the same time would explain to the officials at New Orleans that Dachicoin was a high-ranking Indian of the Adais tribe. "This will be important in my getting a fairer trade for salt and other merchandise", he said. "I would also like for you to request Quitlami, Son of Koanan, who is called the White Chief of the Natchitoches Indians by the French, to insure safe passage among the Indians I might encounter because Quitlami will have the arm band of the Son of a Chief and I the arm band of a conachas of the Adais. These marks of distinction will be observed by those tribes who are not on friendly terms with the French, but who would not wish to arouse an undesirable antagonism between two tribes such as the Adais and the Natchitoches. The letters will safe-guard us from white men who might be inclined to forget the *calumet* of the French and the Caddos of whose Federacy we are members. For this service I will expect a French soldier's coat, one of the things I most desire in life. I will leave two horses at your disposal as a guarantee of my return and my true intention to serve the French. Because of my association with the Caddo Federacy I can be of many uses to the French." The Commandant was no fool. He quickly realized the importance of Dachicoin, and agreed to his wishes even paying Quitlami's expenses in the form of presents from the company merchandise.

To the average reader it would seem that Dachicoin was risking five horses which were of more value on this frontier than the supposed profits of this particular trading trip, but Quitlami revealed to Lotbotiniere that Dachicoin distributed these horses in good hands and those people were obligated to take as good care of them as if the horses belonged to them. Thus Dachicoin was assured of the good care of his animals with no expense to himself.

The canoe or dug-out of Largen was a four-place canoe, which is a boat that required four men to paddle it and would at the same time, besides the human cargo, carry fourteen hundred pounds of freight. Thus equipped Dachicoin and Quitlami set out from Natchitoches to the Distonies on Saline Bayou in Natchitoches Parish, where he traded five of the knives for two hundred gourds of salt, each gourd contained approximately one pound of salt. From Natchitoches he carried the furs of Largen and small gourds of finely chopped matot, ground leaves of the Sassafras tree. This spice was an excellent trade goods of the Natchitoches tribe. The spice, however, was sent by Blondell and was to be exchanged for some personal things for the Commandant. He did, however, pay for Dachicoin's coat out of his own merchandise. Because of the success of the trading trip Dachicoin's name became popular along the frontier. His character was such, that his word was his bond. He never bought any trade goods outright to sell them for a profit as did the French traders. Always he asked for goods on consignment. It was a familiar sight at Natchitoches and at Los Adais to see Dachicoin arrange what he had received for a consignment into three piles — one pile represented the cost of trade goods and one the profits. The one who supplied the merchandise could take his choice of two of the piles, the other went to Dachicoin for his labors.

Dachicoin had taken for his wife, a squaw of the Hasinai said to be a daughter of Bernardino, Chief of that tribe. Upon returning to the Adais, Dachicoin spoke to Largen, who was at the time at the Adais, explaining to him that he wished to be blessed in marriage by a priest just as white men and women were when priests married them. Largen explained to Dachicoin that if he were married by the Church it would be contrary to the beliefs of the Caddos. (The Caddos believed in separations or divorce — that a squaw or man being dissatisfied could separate, the squaw taking the male children and the man the female children. These separations occurred quite often among the different tribes of the Caddos.) At this Dachicoin replied, "A man will have need for only one woman if she is the correct woman for him and a woman needs only one man if he is the correct man for her, my squaw and I understand these things and I, Dachicoin say that it can be no other way." Pierre Largen sponsored the wedding at the Los Adais Church. It is said that Father Margil De Jesus performed the ceremony.

The squaw, or shall I say wife of Dachicoin, was allowed by her husband to ride a horse instead of walking as most Indians required their squaws to do, and, not only that, but to add to her comfort she was seated on a good Spanish saddle, and even had a pack horse to carry such things that a squaw was required to carry. This caused much dissatisfaction among the other squaws and the Indian men alike.

Dachicoin lit the Council Fire of the Adais and when enough of the tribe had gathered, spoke to them. "You of the Adais are cooking in metal pots that I, Dachicoin gave to you. Because all that I have also belongs to my squaw, then she too gave the pots". There was no one to criticize her then, for it is a law of the Caddos that no other person can be concerned in the private affairs of a Caddo family unless invited to do so. If one violates this law then he is to be punished by the elders. "If there are any more envious remarks about my squaw I shall see that the law is fulfilled. What I have said shall now be forgotten, it must not occur again."

At the Natchitoches council fire he berated the Natchitoches in much the same way. Such was the power of Dachicoin that he could demand the obedience of two tribes of Indians.

In 1722 St. Denis returned to Natchitoches replacing Captain Reynaud as Commandante. He, too, was quick to learn the importance of Dachicoin.

In 1723 St. Denis received a demand from Bernardino of the Hasinai for the ransom of a Frenchman. He then sent the small, tin box containing papers of the French officer. St. Denis recognized the name of the officer, a man who once had fought a duel with him. This French officer, Belle-Isle, with St. Denis had attended the Royal School in Paris. They had always seemed to be at odds with each other, and now St. Denis was being asked to pay ransom for him. But St. Denis was not one to hold a grudge, and he knew that Belle-Isle had the makings of a good French officer. He could not bring himself to believe that there was a possibility of Belle-Isle being a deserter and had somehow become a slave of the Indians. Too, he realized the possibility of the Spanish rescuing him, and from gratitude Belle-Isle might have been inclined to offer his services to Spain. St. Denis personally knew French officers in the service of Spain, but now he had the problem of going behind the Spanish Fort at Los Adais to rescue Belle-Isle.

St. Denis sent for Quitlami and had him go to the Adais and bring Dachicoin back with him. When the two Indians returned he sent for Lagross, Largen and Lobotiniere for a conference. All were given the details about Belle-Isle.

The ransom was to be ten French rifles with 100 shots and enough powder to fire those 100 shots for each rifle. This was an impractical and dangerous form of ransom because if the party delivering the rifles should be intercepted by the Spanish they would have grounds to think that the French were trying to supply the Indians with fire arms to be used against them, which could create a disastrous incident on the frontier.

Dachicoin asked if he might speak, and without waiting for a reply, asked St. Denis if he would settle with Bernardino for two rifles and the requested powder and shot. St. Denis would be glad to agree to such a settlement, but continued Dachicoin, "why not turn this trip for ransom into profit?", which caused a raising of eyebrows. All those present were traders and the word "profit" was music to their ears. Dachicoin explained, "Bernardino is a trader and a clever one, and also the father of my squaw. If I go as a member of the ransom party my squaw must also go as she will wish to see her father again. Also this party will need someone to cook for them, she can do that. Bernardino has sent five of his braves and ten extra horses. He fully expects each of those ten extra horses to have something on them. We must send five men to accompany the Hasinais; to send less would show carelessness, to send more would show we were afraid, five men to ride five of the horses sent by Bernardino. We must fix a box of wood the size of one which would contain ten rifles, but insead of rifles it will contain lengths of cane filled with the seeds of watermelons, squash, gourds, corn and beans. The Hasinais are farmers, but because they move around for place to place, staying in one place only long enough to raise and harvest a crop; they are often short of seed, we will also send salt, honey, pecans, hickory nuts, walnuts; these are the things that we have plenty of. In return we will ask for the

Frenchman and horses and some amole root.* The last two things are the cheapest trade-goods of the Hasinais. Bernardino has often admired my French coat and has often tried to trade me for it, but I explained to him that it would be too small for him. If M. Rambin can make a coat the size of the one that would fit M. Largen, then Bernardino would try to trade for it especially if Largen pretends he does not wish to trade for the coat. We will have to explain to Bernardino that we have no extra rifles available but the one I am carrying. The other rifle mentioned will be given to me when I return as payment for my assistance in this trip. My squaw will have among the things necessary for her to take some of the knives from the company store, each of us will also have some knives to trade. We will trade for horses and the amole root and anything else that Bernardino has. Quitlami must tell Bernardino that the coat that M. Largen is wearing is magic and is Largen's trading coat. That when Largent has it on he always makes more profit on his trades. That it would be a great service to the Natchitoches and the Adais if Berdardino could trade Largen out of the coat. So far no one has been able to do this."

The trip from Natchitoches to the Hasinais was roughly about 360 miles.

Immediately on the arrival of the party Bernardino brought the slave Belle-Isle forward and demanded the rifles when he was told that there was only one rifle and it belonged to Dachicoin. He was furious and threatened to kill the slave on the spot. Dachicoin explained that there were many other trade goods of value and things that the Hasinais needed. Largen was not then wearing the coat made by Rambin the tailor.

In true Caddo fashion Bernardino either spit upon or kicked the trade goods offered for Belle-Isle (this was characteristic of the Caddos, any trade goods was treated in such a way as to cheapen it in the eyes of the one offering it for trade. Those things that they wanted most they spurned the most). Each time

---

*The amole root is a species of the yucca plant. When boiled in water, that water used for bathing had the same property as soap and left a fragrant odor on the body of the user.

Bernardino spit on the trade goods, Largen in turn spit upon Belle-Isle, meanwhile telling him in French that this was necessary. Largen picked up a bundle and went into the Hinta-sak of Bernardino. Quickly Quitlami went to Bernardino and explained to him about the coat of Largen. When Largen came back he was strutting and showing off the coat. He explained the designs on the coat, the hawk on one side was an emblem of the Caddos. He was a Caddo because he had taken an Ais Squaw. The Fleur De Lys because he was also French. Twenty buttons, more buttons than on any French or Spanish officer's coat (Rambin had surely done his best work here). Bernardino began wanting to trade for the coat but Largen would hear none of it. Finally Bernardino offered the slave for the coat and explaining that if the slave was a Frenchman and Largen was a Frenchman then they were brothers—surely a brother would give a coat to save his brother's life and if they did not come to an agreement about the coat then the slave was sure to die. Largen then surprised Bernardino by saying he would give the coat if the Chief would given ten horses to the slave and ten horses to him and then trade horses for the other trade goods along with the amole root and some wolf hides. This Barnardino agreed to.

St. Denis was awakened by the sound of thundering hooves. Lobotiniere called to him. St. Denis wiped his eyes as he witnessed the success of the trip — eighty horses, many of them loaded with hides and other merchandise.

After all settlements were made among those who participated on the trip, Belle-Isle told St. Denis of his misfortune. The ship he was on left France in 1718. After they had entered the Gulf of Mexico a storm came up and the ship was blown off course. Then scurvy broke out aboard ship. Finally land was sighted. The ship's captain, believing that the ship was at a point east of Biloxi, put ashore those who were not yet affected, instructing them to go west overland where they would be sure to find the French. However, it must have been west of the Mississippi instead of east of it. Belle-Isle related, "there were five of us, all died except me. In the distance one day I saw a camp fire and went to it. The Indians took me captive and made me a slave. I was with them eighteen months when Bernardino bought me from them. Bernardino could understand a few words of French. He sent the tin box to you. You know the rest. Bernardino, however, did treat me very well". (Belle-Isle was indeed lucky; that ship and its entire crew were never heard of again).

I suggest a toast to Dachicoin, who thought like a Frenchman, spoke like a Spaniard, had all the cunning of an Indian, and the honesty of a Pilgrim. Such was the importance of Dachicoin.

By the year 1740 Belle-Isle had become a power in politics at New Orleans.

In 1737 the Natchitoches tribe was able to ship 350 head of horses to New Orleans as part of its surplus trade-goods, and all because of Dachicoin, a *conachas* of the Adais.

IV

ST. DENIS AND THE SPANISH

In 1724 St. Denis and Almazon affixed the Arroyo Hondo as the boundary between the French and the Spanish. There was also an agreement to allow the French traders, who were to go to the Upper Caddos during the wet season, to pass through the Los Adais area. In this same year Jean Muller was permitted to establish La Post du Bayou Pierre*.

By 1725 St. Denis had won the Spanish commandant over to his point of view and persuaded him to allow free trade in the area. The French were also allowed at Los Adais on Sundays to attend religious services. (The French, up until a few years later, were without the services of a priest at Natchitoches).

Word reached the Viceroy in Mexico City that Almazon was too lenient with the French and that he was actually encouraging open trade with them. In 1730 Almazon was replaced by Don Juan Antonio de Bustillio y Zavalles, who was quick to realize that La Presidio de Los Adais was entirely dependent on the French for its very existence. He sent a letter to the Viceroy to that effect, further advising that the Spanish settlers of the area scarcely produced enough crops to sustain themselves and their families. Zavalles was an experienced military officer and understood the importance of maintaining a modicum of friend-

---

*The present day location is in the King Hill area, which now comprises part of the Simp Russ plantation between Lake End and Ajax, La.

ship on the frontier with the French and the Indians. Zavalles in 1730 issued a land grant to Juan de Mora.*

In 1730 Natchitoches welcomed the arrival of its first French priest, Father Vietry.

In April of 1731 Zavalles received an urgent message from St. Denis saying that the Natchez Indians were on their way to attack the French Post and asked for assistance. Zavalles sent fifteen men, which may just have been enough to help St. Denis gain a victory over the Natchez Indians. One Spaniard lost his life in the battle.

Zavalles was criticized by his Spanish superiors at San Antonio and Mexico City for assisting the French, but Zavalles reasoned that if the French Post had fallen to the Natchez Indians nothing would have prevented the Natchez from attacking the Spanish presidio. There was also the possibility of the Caddos aligning themselves with the Natchez. Such a procedure had often happened among warring Indian tribes against the white man. It is far better, if a battle is to be fought, that it take place in foreign territory. He reasoned that even if the French lost, there would be other Frenchmen to return and settle the land. If the Spanish had gained control of the Adais-Natchitoches frontier their dominance would not have been for long. As a result of this assistance of the Spanish, food and trade-goods from the French became more plentiful and cheaper in price.

Manuel de Sandoval in 1734 replaced Zavalles as Governor of Los Adais. After a few months on the frontier he left and assigned Jose Gonzales as Governor of Los Adais. Zavalles in the meanwhile was being prosecuted at San Antonio de Bexar because of his leniency with the French. An investigation of the conditions on the Spanish frontier proved that Zavalles was correct in his actions. His rank and prestige were restored.

---

*This land grant was where what is commonly called the Fish Pond Bottom by present day inhabitants of the Robeline area. It was referred to later by Dr. John Sibley, an Indian Agent in 1807, as Lagoon de Mora in a letter to Major Porter, Post Commander of Fort Claiborne in Natchitoches.

St. Denis took advantage of the unrest of the Spanish, and in the midst of protests and letter writing, he moved the Post St. Jean Baptiste "one pistol shot" distance to the west bank of the Red River.

Jose Gonzales was commandante of an ill-equipped presidio, the crops were failures and the French had control of the food, but the Spanish always had time for fiesta. And the French came to visit and trade. Much to the discomfort of Gonzales, fraternization became the order of the day.

It was the year 1735, when Chamard erected his home and added a chapel so that civil marriages could be blessed by the priests from Los Adais on their monthly visits. Natchitoches was quite often without the services of a priest at this time. Chamard came to the Natchitoches area in 1730 as an agent and notary for the Company of the Indies. Chamard was a very devout Catholic and was a leader in rebuilding the church which had burned in 1734. He set an excellent example on the frontier for those who were not inclined to attend religious services regularly.

V

DOCTORS AND EARLY MEDICINE — 1722 TO 1744

Medar Jalot had some learning under the direction of Dr. Ambroise Benoist Gendron of Quebec, Canada. Jalot became a member of a party under the guidance of Henri De Tonty (The Iron Hand) that left Quebec in 1710. They came to Biloxi via the Great Lakes, the Illinois River, the Mississippi River, Lake Manchac and Lake Pontchartrain. Jalot was with the St. Denis expedition to Mexico in 1714 as the valet to St. Denis, and in 1722 was listed in the Natchitoches census. Jalot, although not a doctor by title, served the Natchitoches Post in that capacity because of his skill in treating wounds and body sores. Jalot also had knowledge of many Indian remedies for the sicknesses of the country.

It was the custom at this time for Kings to issue certificates to men of the medical profession, designating them as *Docteur du Roi*, Doctor of the King. Doctors who would accept such a commission for frontier duty would receive a year's salary in advance, clothing, a chest of medicine, an allotment of paper, note books and the personal best wishes of the King. The physician would then in turn be obliged to render his services free to the militia and others connected with the service of a post and the Indians of the surrounding area. The post of his designated-location would place at the doctor's disposal, an office, lodging and food at the officers' table. Transportation was obligingly supplied by the King, "a one way ticket."

To the young Doctor who had thus qualified himself this would seem to be a golden opportunity. Dr. Le Beau was the first to arrive at the Natchitoches post. He was the first Doctor to realize that this golden opportunity did not supply medium-of-exchange. The post personnel, their wives and children were exempt from payment for his services. All of the inhabitants and their families supplied the post with food and produce, so they were also exempt as were the Indians. The doctor knew that he would have to wait two years before he would receive his next salary from the King. He could receive payment for his services to the Spanish at Los Adais, but traffic with the Spanish was forbidden. He was soon to realize that the first year's pay that had been issued would only buy three pairs of pants at Rambin's Tailor shop . . . and that Rambin was making his livelihood by redoing old clothing rather than tailoring new garments. Too, he was duty bound to stay one year in the service to fulfill his obligation to the Crown. By not doing so he was subject to arrest. Needless to say, after his year was up Dr. Le Beau resigned his commission and struck out on his own.

In 1727 Dr. Alexander was the next "Docteur du Roi" to arrive in Natchitoches. He was killed in a duel by Captain Jentzen, a Swedish officer in the service of the King of France.

In 1730 Dr. Godeau arrived with a King's Commission. He wed the Widow Brossilier, and adopted his two-year-old step-daughter. The Widow Brossilier had land, and so this doctor became a farmer and notary, with his medical profession becoming a sideline.

The people of the Natchitoches area did not like the idea of having to pay for doctor's services. Doctor Godeau had, after his first year resigned his commission, and now could charge legally for his services. They waited but no new Docteur du Roi arrived.

Dr. Godeau was at the Natchitoches Post at the time of the Natchez Indian attack. In this two-months war on the Natchitoches frontier the Doctor won the friendship of the fifteen Spaniards who assisted in the defense of the French Post. In 1733 Dr. Godeau travelled to the Adais Post on Saturdays and Sundays to render his services to the Spanish, and to attend mass on Sunday. Thus, in the Robeline area was set up the first form of medical clinic in all the territory later comprised in the Louisiana Purchase. The Spanish had money to pay for professional services which naturally attracted men of any profession.

The people's voice must have been heard, for the Good King Louis XV sent in 1737 Dr. Tontin. By this time King Louis must have decided that it was easier to send new doctors each year as soon as they were qualified *medecins*. He realized that the "one way ticket" was just another way to populate Louisiana with learned men. Doctor Pain (or Payne) was sent in 1738, Doctor Jaubaer in 1739, and Doctor Bonnafons in 1740.

So now it was Dr.Bonnafons turn to match his wits with this French frontier. In sizing up his predicament Dr. Bonnafons found that the recognized occupations listed on the post roster as ones that were to obtain free medical service were: Trappers, Traders, Commercial Hunters and Fishermen, Druggists, Farmers, Blacksmiths, Store owners, Tailors, Bakers, Carpenters, Gunsmiths, Butchers, Soldiers and the Indians. The good commandante, Louis Juchereau de St. Denis, saw to it that all of these men obtained their just share of the Post business. I feel sure, too, that the doctors, Pain, Jambare and Tontin advised Doctor Bonnafons what to expect. This doctor, however, had the wits to fit the occasion. He demanded of St. Denis that because the office space inside the fort was too small, that a building be erected outside the fort for his home and office. He showed the commandante that according to the rights ennumerated in his commission that the Post Commander must furnish him with these suitable conveniences. St. Denis complied with the doctor's demands.

Dr. Bonnafons became a barber and for this privilege he paid a license. Being a barber he was allowed to sell drugs. The druggist was part of the Grocery Guild, so that he was now qualified to sell "stuffs" (bolts of uncut cloth). Sieur Ignace Antee, a farmer and part-time cobbler, was encouraged to erect a lean-to on the opposite side of the doctor's building. Because he had assisted Laignon and Antee to erect their lean-tos, Dr. Bonnafons considered himself a carpenter. He informed Jacques

Turpeax, a soldier and baker at the Natchitoches Post, that he would purchase the surplus bread which was baked and not used by the militia, thus furnishing quick lunches for weary, hungry travelers. Because the Doctor was in the grocery business, he could sell wine which went well with the cheese brought to the French Post by the inhabitants of Campti.

One must realize that we are at a time between the dates 1740 and 1744, because St. Denis died in 1744, and that the location of Dr. Bonnafons' building would have been near the new fort which had been erected by St. Denis "one pistol shot to the west" from the location of the Fort St. Jean Baptiste as shown on Breutin's Map of 1722. This placed the new fort in the environs of what was later the American cemetery. As to the location of Dr. Bonnafons' building we have this clue. In his ledger he states that he obtained land adjoining his from Duplessis. On Breutin's map the Duplessis land would have been in the vicinity of the south bank of Bayou Amulet near G. W. Black's Grocery and Market. Also, in this same area along Bayou Amulet the traders coming to Natchitoches tethered their mules.

Having obtained this land adjoining his building, Dr. Bonnafons erected a blacksmith shop for Jean Baptist Marin. As the doctor's business grew, so did the buildings and the good doctor had his eye out for more business and reasoned that "where their is a demand, there should be a supply".

About 20 years preceding Dr. Bonnafons' arrival in Natchitoches, some of the farmers had obtained slaves from New Orleans. The slaves, coming directly from Africa, believed in voodoo, and for a generation had sold their charms, amulets, love potions and cure-all charms to the Indians, as well as the white inhabitants.

Dr. Bonnafons, being a druggist and grocer was allowed, according to the Drug Guild, to sell notions. So he added a trinket department to his store which had such items as earrings, necklaces, mirrors and of course the voodoo charms. Bonnafons reasoned that the local natives and inhabitants might just as well have the imported kind from New Orleans where the voodoo charm-makers were more skilled and the charms had more power. He reasoned with himself that according to law, slaves were not allowed to have money or engage in a business which would supply them with money. So he decided to put them out of business. Naturally Dr. Bonnafons told his customers that he did not believe in voodoo, that he was a doctor and that only a doctor could cure illnesses — that the charms were just novelties and that some people bought them in ignorance.

Commercial traders with the Indians who bought such trinkets from Dr. Bonnafons at a discount were Jean Camion, Nicholas and Jean Lassard, Pierre Gaigne, Lantallac, Nicholas Tibaud, Francois Gueno, De Lima of Los Adais, Francois Moreau, Jean Robalet, Louis Barme, Joseph Le Douc, Jean Baptiste Derbonne, Le Bomme, Henri Vidol and Pierre Bossier. By supplying these traders Dr. Bonnafons became the first wholesaler of merchandise in the Natchitoches section.

As the following bill testifies, Dr. Louis Bonnafons served the Natchitoches area well. The bill concerns the services rendered to Pierre Fausse's young son.

1. Pour *6* bouttiles de quillendive* per l'order du chirurgiens.
2. Pour *6* denier (6 articles of merchandise.)
3. Pour 12 boutilles d'eau de vie. (Brandy used as a sedative to settle nerves and upset stomach.)
4. Pour *6* bouttiles de medecine laxatif (laxatives).
5. Pour le cerceuil de defuma. (For making the coffin.)

The child was given 6 bottles of nausea medicine, 12 bottles of brandy (that is, if the child was given all of the brandy — he may have had help in disposing of this medicine) and 6 bottles of laxatives. This was enough of such medicine to kill any patient. Dr. Bonnafons, being the doctor in attendance, would also be the first to know of the child's death. Thus being a carpenter he was also a cabinet maker which made him a coffin-maker. Thus Dr. Bonnafons was also an undertaker.

---

*This medicine became popular among the doctors at that time according to the reference of an old book at the office of the late Dr. J. N. Brown of Campti, Louisiana. *Quillendive* meant seeds of certain plants, not just one particular plant or herb. When administered, the medicine caused nausea.

From Dr. Louis Bonnafons' ledger, covering a six-year period from 1741 to 1747, come these names and families: Joseph Lattier, soldier; Claud Bertrand, soldier; Jean La Berry, soldier; Louis Juchereau de St. Denis family; Antoine Chesneau family; Michel Chesneau family; Pierre Baillio, soldier; Vencient Perrier family; Remi Possiot family; Louis Rachal family; Gaspard Barbier, brother of Madam Cheveret — "bought violin sold to me by Bartholmey Rachal"; Joseph Robideux (Robeaux), one powder horn; Jean Baptiste Gonnin, carpenter; Francois Gurno, carpenter; Pierre Allarg, carpenter; Pierre Mercer, farmer; Andre Barringer, farmer; Remi Possiot, soldier; Fancois Langlois, soldier; Edwardo Lattier, soldier-farmer; Louis Badin, farmer; Andries Rambin family; Louis Rambin family; Madam de La Chaise. There were many more, but to list them would be a repetition of names mentioned earlier in this book.

Dr. Louis Bonnafons died in 1759. He never married. His ledger brings out but one important fact: Natchitoches and El Camino Real area has always had possibilities for the right sort of man. Likewise, these so-called, one-stop, shopping centers are nothing new to our country. Too, during this early period of the Natchitoches community there was a form of socialized medicine, which proved even at this early period a doctor could not exist by merely depending on his chosen profession for a livelihood when controlled or limited by the state.

VI

ROMANCE AT LOS ADAIS

There was quite a stir on the fine spring morning of April 8, 1735 at Los Adais. Senorita Victoria Gonzales, daughter of the Lieutenant Governor of this Spanish presidio, had eloped with a Frenchman, Jean Baptista DerBonne, assisted by two other Frenchmen of the Post St. Jean Baptiste des Natchitoches after the High Mass that Sunday. Governor Gonzales, holding office during the absence of Governor Manuel de Sandoval, and Reverend Padre Ignacio Certa were talking when word of the elopment was brought. A searching party was immediately organized but was unsuccessful in capturing the culprits.

The next day Gonzales wrote a letter to his superiors, stating the above details and adding that, even though DerBonne was a French officer and a gentleman, he had refused permission for the marriage. He was so infuriated that he disowned his daughter, thereby wishing to show to the officials over him that he had nothing to do with this matter. However, he did suspect Padre Certa and his brother-in-law Juan de Mora, because both had intervened in DerBonne's behalf. He also added that de Mora was in jail and at present he had not decided what to do with him. He received word that the party arrived in Natchitoches at midnight, and Father Pierre Vietry, a priest of the Jesuit Order, had married Victoria and DerBonne immediately, thus violating the laws of the Catholic Faith. He wrote: "As you know the banns of bethrothed have to be announced at three Sunday Services before the wedding. I am told that the elopers traveled by pirogue, going from arroyo to arroyo and finally reaching the Red River and then on to Natchitoches, which explains why our land searching-party did not find them. Padre Vallejo of the Mission Margil de Los Adais is going to Natchitoches to request wine so necessary in the procedure of the Mass. I am sure Victoria will accompany him back to Los Adais to get her things and the family blessing. Now that she has been married by the Church there is nothing I can do. She is seventeen and of marriageable age."

The two nationalities had much to say to each other about this wonderful new topic of conversation. The Spanish would give credit to Victoria for planning the whole thing, after all a woman of Victoria's intelligence must have planned it because certainly a Frenchman could not have had the head for such clever thinking — DerBonne was just the lucky one who won her heart. The French would say that DerBonne was a sly one, that he had stolen Victoria from under their very eyes. The stupid Spanish bachelors, allowing such a pretty prize as Victoria to slip away from them. And so the talk went, but there has to be a formula for each and every elopement that is successful.

Now in this case, take three bayous, a little river and a larger river, mix with one uncle, a willing duenna, two willing assistants, two understanding priests, a friend. Add a handsome French officer, a beautiful senorita and an irate father. Then allow a certain amount of time for observation to turn into fascination, watch closely as fascination develops into desire and desire materializes into love, then you will have the correct ingredients for a successful elopement. So explains the material gathered from John Eskew, Belisle, J. Fair Hardin, Ross Phares and Poitre-Babinsik. All of these authors have shed some light on this incident.

Now, as a certain character would say, let's add up the facts.

Jean Baptist Der Bonne or Derbonne as the French would write it, was an officer at the French Post, Jean Baptist Des Natchitoches. The Spanish Post, Del Presidio Neustra Senora del Pilar de Los Adais, was roughly 17 miles due west. The dividing boundary was the Arroyo Hondo, a small stream that ran roughly north and south midway between these two outposts.

True, both nationalities respected this boundary to a certain extent, that is they visited openly but hid their trading with each other.

The Spanish had use of the good Doctor Payne (Pain), the post Doctor at Natchitoches, in return the Spanish Fiesta was open to all. If a Frenchman visited the Spanish Church for Mass or Confession he was very welcome.

Father Ignacio Certa admitted in one of his letters that he had spoken to Gonzales in behalf of Der Bonne. Certainly this priest must have approved of the Frenchman or he would not have intervened for him.

The foster brother of Gonzales's wife, Juan de Mora, was a very good friend of Der Bonne because he helped and was put into prison because of the incident. Even this imprisonment was a sham, as De Mora could have gone to the post at Natchitoches a guest of DerBonne. He could have left immediately after the two eloped and with a fast horse, reached Natchitoches well ahead of any searchers. I believe de Mora remained at Los Adais and allowed himself to be imprisoned so that his brother-in-law, Gonzales, might save face with his superiors in Mexico and the Tejas country. There are no records revealing a trial or punishment of Juan de Mora. One thing is certain, there was a food and clothing shortage at Los Adais and de Mora was one of the Spaniards who was on very good terms with the French officer, DerBonne. And DerBonne, being an officer, would have enough influence at the French post at Natchitoches to assist the Spanish traders in getting more reasonable bargains when purchasing food and clothing there. Too, DerBonne being a French officer, as a side line, also was a trader among the Indians and certainly with the Spanish. Now that the Frenchman had taken a Spanish wife and she being the daughter of Gonzalez, the Gonzalez family would certainly profit by this marriage. The deals, however, having been transacted through DerBonne and De Mora and both men now being of the Gonzalez family would leave the Lieutenant Governor in the clear as far as his superiors were concerned.

The duenna (chaperone) of Victoria Gonzalez must have assisted the two lovers, reasoning that the duties of a duenna, are to look after her charge's morals and religious training and to teach her things she must know concerning her social standing and her responsibilities to her family in respect to marriage. A duenna, therefore accepted or rejected those who wished to court her charge. Quite often the duenna had to be won as well as the young senorita. The chaperone's duty was to chanel her young charge's affections and thoughts toward the suitor considered most able to support the young lady in the manner to which she was accustomed; but the duenna would also observe the suitors that the senorita liked best, and by elimination, to these she thought most suitable, certain privileges would be allowed. In this case the suitor was DerBonne. Now came the time for observation to turn into fascination. To watch closely as fascination develops into desire, and then when desire materializes into love, arrangements must be made so that the wedding can be solemnized. The duenna or chaperon was also a match-maker.

Now for allowing those certain privileges. At a fiesta at Los Adais, DerBonne and Victoria danced, and after a while walked out into the patio for a breath of fresh air. The man, being a gentleman, would not on first meeting attempt to guide his companion to a darkened shadowy spot for closer conversation. The duenna naturally followed and observed at a discreet distance. She would locate herself at such vantage point where she could see and yet not be seen.

At Church on Sunday, DerBonne having received an invitation from de Mora, with de Mora advising DerBonne to be there early, arrangements were made so that DerBonne sat next to Victoria, with the duenna on one side of the couple and deMora on the other. Perhaps at sometime during the services of the Mass the duenna suggested a walk in a certain direction, making sure that DerBonne overheard the suggestion intended for Victoria. Just to be sure, immediately after the Church Services de Mora would suggest a stroll before eating the noon meal, and, as if by chance both parties met at some point on a secluded footpath, the young couple would find that for the moment they were alone and unobserved, while the elderly couple was engaged in some topic of conversation. Now for a quick embrace and kiss while the old duenna was not looking. To these well planned, or chance meetings as the young couple thought, surely fate was lending a helping hand. So fascination turns into desire and desire into love. Now to ask for her hand in marriage (the old duenna and de Mora must have felt proud of themselves.) Der Bonne asked the father, Jose Gonzalez, but the irate father refused. Then the priest, Father Ignacio Certa, interceded on behalf of DerBonne. Another refusal as the obdurate father explained that the Spanish authorities would not permit such a thing on the frontier. After all, the Spanish and the French were rivals here, and such a marriage might even lead to war among the two nationalities at these outposts of empire.

DerBonne was well aware of the dire consequences that might result from the marriage and without a doubt had discussed the situation with his Commandante, St. Denis. Now, Louis Juchereau de St. Denis was one of the slyest and most commercial-minded men who ever trod the soil of Natchitoches, certainly the most adventurous. Without accusing him of entering into a conspiracy, he evaluated the circumstances concerning this elopement, and weighed the risks of the outcome.

First, DerBonne was a good French soldier and officer and if he were to get married this would bring about family ties on the frontier, which would keep him in the Natchitoches district (quite often when a soldier's enlistment expired he left the Natchitoches area for greener pastures). DerBonne would settle land nearby so that his wife to be would be near her own people. Eventually when his enlistment expired, the French would have an experienced officer in this area without having to pay for his services. DerBonne was also a trader, and his supplies were furnished by the store at the Natchitoches post and St. Denis received a commission on all merchandise sold at the post as well as on all trade merchandise sent back to New Orleans. This marriage between DerBonne and the daughter of a high ranking official at Los Adais would naturally bring on better trade relations, even if it was to be effected in a slightly underhand way.

Secondly, St. Denis understood the love of a Spanish parent wishing to see his offspring happily married. He probably thought of his own marriage to Manuella and how her family risked all their worldly possessions and position of office to protect his marriage into the Don Diego Ramone family. The Spanish, to be sure, had their faults, but also they must be commended for their forgiving and understanding nature when the welfare of their families was concerned. In this respect Jose Gonzalez, the Lieutenant Governor of Los Adais, would be no exception. He knew that this man would have to do a great deal of letter writing and pretending but in the end would be a forgiving father-in-law. St. Denis, after weighing the risks, secretly consented to lend his support to this marriage. Even if the risks had been greater St. Denis would have given his consent because his whole life, if one studies it carefully, was full of risks and intrigue. One more incident would have made no difference to him. The fact is that he probably enjoyed the entire situation, for this affair would bring a new topic of interest and conversation to the dull life of the frontier.

The whole procedure of the successful elopement suggests the cool, calculating mind of one such as St. Denis possessed, not the flustrated mind of a young lover.

Let us examine the water-route that these two elopers traveled: The Arroyo Adais, a small stream of water that ran near the Presidio De Los Adais and then into the Bayou Mayoux. This bayou ran into La Petite Rigolet (Little River, as it is known today) in turn ran into Bayou Pierre, which drained into Red River (just above Grande Ecore) flowed past the French fort at Natchitoches. The distance traveled would be about twenty-four miles.

Governor Gonzalez's letter states that DerBonne and two Frenchmen ran off with his daughter. These two Frenchmen would have to be hand-picked men capable of carrying out an assignment without a flaw. Men who could stand the rigors of twenty-four miles of continuous paddling, part of the time being in the black of the night, men who could be trusted to keep their mouths shut, and above all men who were not afraid of danger for which there would be no profit to them and certain imprisonment if they were caught. Evidently the post at Natchitoches had two such men. However, their names are not mentioned. So by process of elimination of the known inhabitants of Natchitoches at this time let's see if we can determine who these two men were. But first, one most important point that should be brought out, because as they were to travel by water there could be no risk of a drowning, especially of the girl — if this were to happen war would certainly follow. The inhabitants of Natchitoches in 1736 were: St. Denis, Commandante, his wife, Manuella and his children; Pierre Largen, trader, married to an Ais Indian maiden; Lt. Basset next in command; Lobotiniere, trader and farmer, married; Duterpints, soldier and baker for the post; Jean Lagross, trader and merchant, settled across the river from Campti; Dr. Payne (Pain), Doctor and Notary, married; Jean Baptista Deherbonne (BerBonne, Derbon, Derbonne); Lt. Gautren, married; Lafreniere, soldier; Joseph La Duc, soldier; Prudhomme, planter and trader, married; Sieur Barme, store keeper, married; Jacques De La Chase, government storekeeper, married; P. Duplessis, Notary, married; Father Pierre Vietry, Jesuit Priest; Sieur Bacque, farmer, married; Pierre Mercer, farmer; Andre Berrange, farmer; Antoine Germaine, soldier; Juan Biseros, merchant, married; Antonio Charbonnet, merchant; Gilbert Maxent, merchant; Pierre Gaignie, trader, married; Nicholas Tibaud, trader; Paul Muller, soldier; the two Barberousses, hunters contracted to supply meat for the Post; LaRenaudiere, a miller; Rambin, a tailor, married; The Dupress brothers, hunters and trappers; DeLame, storekeeper and trader; Jean Layssard and Nicholas Layssard, brothers, soldiers and traders; Lantallic, farmer and trader; Sieur Badin, farmer, trader and storekeeper; Francois Lemoine, soldier in love with Victoria Emanuella Garcia; Sieur Jambare, doctor.

According to a 1735 census there were only 32 people at Natchitoches, however, this must have meant the personnel of the Post St. Jean Baptist. It will be noticed that there were many traders listed, undoubtedly many of these were also soldiers, but not listed as soldiers, because a soldiers pay was so small, and that they were paid only once a year, if at all. Many of them drew from the Army Post Exchange and sold this merchandise either to the Indians or the Spaniards, who seemed to have many gold coins, but there the army post had nothing to sell them. The reason being that Los Adais was too remote from its base of supplies.

Of all the names listed, the two most likely to have assisted DerBonne would have been Francois Lemoine and Jean Lagrosse. I give these reasons — Francois Lemoine was young, strong and ablebodied or he would not have been a soldier. He was in love with a Spaniard, Victorie Emanuello Garcia. Therefore, if someone was willing to break the barrier between the two nations he might profit by assisting and observing the outcome. Jean Lagross, Indian trader had married a Caddo maiden of the Ais tribe. By so doing he was recognized as a member and friend of the Caddo federation of which the Adais Indians at Los Adais was also a tribe of this federation. This being the case the Adais would not take part in a search for a member of their own nation if their assistance was requested by the Governor of the Spanish Fort. Lagross had been with St. Denis during his stay in Mexico, he had a good knowledge of the Spaniard's abilities, and too, Lagross had many friends among the Spanish. Being a trader he had traveled this water route many times. His skilled hands would surely be the ones to steer the pirogue safely back to Natchitoches.

The good friends, St. Denis and Manuella, would have met the boat when it arrived at Natchitoches. Manuella would not have missed this wedding for anything. After all Victoria was of her own people and who in Natchitoches could best represent her.

Now for the part of Gonzalez's letter stating that a priest could not marry a couple without the proper notices of the betrothal being read on three consecutive Sundays. This is true in most cases, but, there is an old saying that the French always had a way for everything, and so in this case they had a way which was recognized by the Church. Due to the shortage of priests in Louisiana there was a ceremony of marriage called "jumping the broom" and in the eyes of witnesess this was considered a just and true marriage. The couple vowed that the wedding would be solemnized as soon as a priest was available (Quite often in recent years this procedure was looked upon as a joke but in the year 1735 in Louisiana it was no joking matter). Here, too, a time element was necessary. Possibly somewhere enroute to Natchitoches this party pulled the boat onto the bank long enough to make a broom of switch cane and the two witnesses, Lagrosse and Lemoine, watched as DerBonne and Victoria jumped the broom. This was necessary. You will note that the wedding took place after mid-night or right at mid-night, the beginning of another day. When the couple told Father Vietry that they had jumped the broom yesterday they did not lie, they had witnesses to prove it. Father Pierre Vietry had no choice but to marry them.

Just so you do not get the wrong impression of Jose Gonzalez you should know that in his letter he states that Padre Vallejo was going to Natchitoches the next day and that Victoria would return with him to receive blessings of her family. Later maps of Natchitoches show that DerBonne owned more land than St. Denis, the Commandante of the Natchitoches Post. Gonzalez could have refused Victoria her dowry because she eloped. Either she got the dowry or DerBonne was an excellent trader. With twenty eight known competitors in the same profession, I believe he got the dowry, and Papa Gonzalez saved face and his position by the elopement happening as it did. And, too, I believe Jose could have written that letter before the elopement and put down the facts just as they occurred.

In July of the same year Francois Lemoine married Victoria Manuella Garcia. And so . . . the Arroyo Honda barrier came down.

VII

INCIDENTS OF THE YEARS, 1735 - 1742

In 1735 Justine de Louche was the first to settle in the area of Cloutierville, Louisiana.

In 1736 Manuel Flores and Carlos Bustimento demanded the same privileges allowed Sanchez, that the Spanish Governor of Los Adais give them title to their land. This was granted and soon to follow were grants to Solice, Toro, Rodriguez, Martinez and Garcia. These family men soon became independent and also became traders among the Indians.

In this same year Benites Franquis de Lugo replaced Sandoval as Governor of Los Adais. An old enemy of Sandoval, he placed him under arrest and stripped the ex-governor of his wealth and rank. He was charged with deserting the post at Los Adais and going to live at San Antonio de Bexar, thereby neglecting the duties of his office; and for recognizing the Arroyo Hondo boundary instead of the west bank of the Red River, thus allowing the French to build a new fort on that side of the Red River.

The friends of Sandoval appealed to the Viceroy to send witnesses to Los Adais to investigate the charges of Governor Lugo.

In 1737 Fernandez de Jauregui Y Urritgua, who was at that time Governor of Nueva Leon, a region which adjoined the Coahuila and Tejas country, came to Los Adais as a *visatador* (witness). He questioned the population, visited the post at Natchitoches and made inquiries there. Lieutenant Gonzalez explained the conditions of the presidio, the shortage of manpower and food and how nearly all the necessities necessary to sustain life had to be obtained from the French.

Urritgua left Prudincio de Orbito as temporary governor, arrested Lugo, sent a message back to the Viceroy clearing Sandavol of all charges and requesting that the prisoner be restored to his position. In the same year San Antonious Bazaterra was sent as Governor of Los Adais and all of the Texas Region. Bazaterra was a merchant from Saltillo in Mexico, and he used his new position to transport his personal merchandise to the Adais frontier. He demanded that the Spanish cease trading with the French.

In April, 1738, he detained and arrested Jean Lagross, a French trader en-route to the Upper Caddos on the big bend of the Red River. According to the Arroyo Hondo agreement between Sandavol and St. Denis, the French traders were to be allowed to pass through the Spanish held Adais land during the wet season. Jean Lagross had a passport to that effect, but Bazaterra refused to recognize the passport and had Lagross' merchandise burned in front of witnesses.

Word of his action soon reached St. Denis and messages were sent to Los Adais, to San Antonio and to Mexico City, by means of Indian carriers. Bazaterra was accused of trouble making and charged with making advances toward Lagross' wife, who, although an Indian, had been legally wed to Lagross at La Mission Senora de Guadelupe at Nacogdoches. Therefore she was a French woman and had been recognized as such by the French at Natchitoches and by the Spanish at Los Adais since her wedding. St. Denis also reminded the Spanish officials that due to the fact that Lagross had taken an Ais maiden for his wife, in the eyes of the Caddo Federation of Indians, Lagross was a Caddo according to the Indian's viewpoint, therefore, this injustice could lead to serious trouble if the Frenchman were not compensated for his loss. Much to the disappointment of Bazaterra, he was ordered to pay Lagross for his merchandise out of his own pocket. "Such", remarked St. Denis, "is the power of the pen".

Bazaterra, however, in spite of his difficulties, piled up the equivalent of forty thousand dollars during his nearly four-year tenure as Governor on the Adais frontier. It must be said on his behalf that he was an excellent tradesman. St. Denis admitted that he was glad to see him leave.

In 1741 Thomas Phillip Winthuisin replaced Bazaterra as Governor of Los Adais. The new governor was a civilian and lacking in the knowledge of the military. This in itself presented a dangerous situation on the Adais frontier. The inhabitants requested that a man of the military be sent to Los Adais.

And in 1742 the talk of the year was how two ex-French soldiers, Lavespere and Brossilier, maintained *travasser* (a kind of flat boat) service from New Orleans to Natchitoches, bringing additional medical supplies to Dr. Bonnafons. These two men had rigged their boat with pulleys which enabled them to pull the boat through the shallow places in the river at low-water stage.

VIII

THE THREE CABINS

Jose Guiterez, a *mestizo* (a person of mixed Indian and Spanish blood) was returning from Natchitoches after having visited the store of Dr. Bonnafons. As he descended the trail down the side of Grand Montania he allowed his horse to pick its way. At the foot of this high hill a small creek flowed called the Arroyo Hondo and at the bank of the small creek he must rest his animal for a while before continuing on to his home near the Presidio de Los Adais. The spring of the year 1742 had been a very trying and wet year, the Arroyo Hondo would be wider now because of so much rainfall. He always felt good when he reached this small rivulet, considered the half-way distance from Los Adais to Natchitoches, for in his mind he felt he was more than half-way home.

As Guiterez rested he thought of his horse, a beautiful stallion. He often wondered if the Indian who had traded the mare, which was with foal at the time and later delivered this colt, envied him now because of the trade. Certainly many of the French officers at Natchitoches and Los Adais had tried to buy the animal, but Jose would always refuse to consider even talking of a trade or sale. Not only because he was such a fine animal, he loved the horse, *El Trumpitero,* named so because of the shrill whinnies the horse voiced when a female of his species was in his vicinity. And Jose had reaped generous profits in stud fees. The horse had made quite a name for himself and for his owner, Jose Guiterez.

The year before the young Spaniard had been sent to the Presidio de San Antonio de Bexar to deliver a message from the Governor, Winthusin, to the alvarez of San Antonio de Bexar asking his opinion about paying the French trader, Jean Lagross, for goods that had been confiscated by the former Governor of Los Adais, Bazaterra, after he had granted a passport to the Frenchman to travel through the Spanish territory when going to trade with the Caddos on upper Red River.

The alvarez at San Antonio de Bexar did not see the situation as clearly as did the Governor of Los Adais and was inclined to advise against paying Lagross. He first asked Guiterez's opinion concerning the contents of the message because he was the only one present who would know some of the events that led to the new Governor of Los Adais' request. Guiterez explained to the alvarez that this particular situation was important because the French trader had married an Ais Indian maiden, therefore, in the eyes of all of the Caddo tribes he was considered a Caddo and the whole Caddo Federacy might take offense if the goods were not paid for; that on the Adais frontier it was necessary to maintain friendly relations with the French in order to purchase much-needed food supplies for the Spanish troops at el Presidio de Los Adais. Jean Lagross was one of the Frenchmen with the Ramone Domingo expedition that established the Spanish missions as far as the Nacogdoches Indians, and from that year, 1716, he had traded among the Indians of this frontier. For the last twenty-five years he had been known favorably in all this country.

"This is no ordinary French trader but one who is loved by the Spanish, French and the Indians, it is best to pay him for his merchandise."

El Trumpitero had carried his master to San Antonio de Bexar and back to Los Adais in less than three weeks, a distance of over a thousand miles. Another time the horse went to Natchitoches and back to Los Adais for medicine for a sick soldier, over thirty miles, in five hours. Because of his horse Guiterez had become the official messenger of Los Adais, which had by now realized the importance of his horse. The children at Los Adais greeted the horse and waved at him as if the animal was a human being. Jose and his horse were such a common sight at Natchitoches even inside the post.

On each occasion when he arrived at Natchitoches he always felt obliged to go by the house of St. Denis, whose wife was Spanish, and tell her of the news at Los Adais. He was likewise welcomed at the house of Jean Baptist DerBonne who had wed Victoria Gonzalez, the daughter of a past governor of Los Adais. Another hospitable friend, Francois Lemoine, was a cousin of Louis Juchereau de St. Denis of the Lemoyne family as were Iberville and Bienville. This young French soldier had married Victoria Emmanuella Garcia, the daughter of a Spanish sergeant of the Presidio at Los Adais. Thus Jose Guiterez was most welcome at these three homes of Frenchmen in Natchitoches. Aside from bringing news to these three Spanish ladies, they in turn found out through Guiterez what the needs of the women of Los Adais were and then purchased these necessities for them from the stores at Natchitoches because trade between the two posts was forbidden. As a result the Spanish women at Los Adais did their trading through the Spanish women at Natchitoches, which custom continued even when trade between the two posts was not forbidden.

As Jose sat on the bank of the Arroyo Hondo admiring his horse, he leaned against the trunk of a tall, slender tree and began to think about his future. For a long time he had felt that there was something lacking in his life but he had not been able to put his finger on the cause of his unrest. He questioned himself about his status in life, concerning his accomplishments and his ability to support himself and his parents, and came to the conclusion he needed a wife and property of his own — either a farm or a business of some kind. He knew that his parents did not need support from him and that his older brothers actually operated the small rancho and farm — they were all married and therefore would continue to remain on the family estate. According to the custom of the times, the oldest brother would inherit the estate, that is the profits from the operation of it. He, Jose Guiterez, decided he would strike out for himself, perhaps engaging in some kind of business for he did not like rancho or farm work. Being a soldier had too many disadvantages. True, in the end after an enlistment period, a soldier was given a certain amount of land, farm animals and equipment. He could get them from his own family if he needed them. Being a settler on a frontier was just as important as being a soldier, each in his own way was serving the purpose of making the frontier secure.

There was a chatter of birds in the tree tops just above his head which broke his train of thought and brought him back to reality. As he looked upward Jose marvelled at the size and the straightness of the trees from which the chatter of the birds had come. Then he noticed how nearly all the trees were of uniform size, straight, and all nearly sixty feet high. Here was definitely cabin material and even in this small grove there were enough such trees to make several cabins. Odd, he thought, he had passed this place many times and did not notice the surroundings as he did this day. As his thoughts raced ahead he rembered that he had stopped to rest, almost always everyone else who passed this way also stopped. Here would be the place to establish some sort of tavern, wine shop or eating place. Why, he wondered, had not someone thought of this before, to erect such a place here on the Arroyo Hondo where people must pass and where they always stop to rest a while. Jose reasoned that the wine shop, tavern and inn, must be available for the French, Spanish and Indian trade, and regardless of what would be traded to him, whether furs or trade goods, sooner or later he could turn them into gold and silver. Now, for obtaining the land. The east side of the Arroyo Hondo, where he intended to establish this new business, belonged to the French. According to an agreement between St. Denis and Governor Almazon in 1724, the dividing line between the French and Spanish would be the Arroyo Hondo instead of the west bank of the Red River as previously claimed by the Spanish. To acquire this deed would require some tact. First, he would get the land and then a wife who could be able to help him operate his business. Which nationality owned this land on the east bank of the Arroyo Hondo made no difference. Jose decided that he would get a grant-title from both representatives of their respective governments. It would be interesting to see if he, a Spaniard, might obtain a land grant from the French, too, and if this could be done, it would be quite a feather in his hat, making him more popular among his Spanish friends.

The grove of trees and the slight rise of the earth there formed a sort of flat shelf. The land was about ninety *toises* (540 feet) square and extended from the Arroyo Hondo to the base of Grand Montania, and the trail leading up the face of Grand Montania divided the land. This was a good feature and he would ask for all land on each side of the trail so that no one else could come in and establish another business near this resting place and be his competitor.

Guiterez was excited. Even he, with no experience in the operation of such a tavern, could see the immediate success of it.

El Trumpitero with a loud whinney announced the presence of other horses in the vicinity, and, as Jose looked across the Arroyo Hondo, he could see a small pack train composed of eight horses and three riders. As the train neared and the animals began to ford the stream he recognized the party of Jean Lagross with his Ais squaw wife, Isobel, and their daughter, Francine Manuella, named "Manuella" to honor Madam St. Denis, who was her godmother.

Because of so much rainfall the water of the stream was swift and deep, and Jose rode El Trumpitero out to the ford to offer assistance to the party if needed.

One thing that both the French and Spanish had learned from the Indians was the maintenance of markers on fordable streams such the the Arroyo Hondo. Slender, cypress poles were placed in a line and at intervals across the stream, each pole was painted in rings of green, yellow and red; the red being at the top of the pole. By looking at the poles and their markings the depth of the water could be ascertained. The markers were on each side of the crossing marking the now submerged trail. This ford crossing of the Arroyo Hondo was only about sixty feet from bank to bank, but on occasion it could be very dangerous if one were not careful and allowed the current to get the upper hand. The water at this time had risen past the red markings on the poles, denoting the stream to be nearly six feet deep and warning that fording it would be dangerous. Jose had noticed the markings and this was the reason that he rode his horse part way out into the water.

Jose shouted across to Lagross to have the women mount the largest horses, and in the meantime he cast his long rawhide rope to Lagross. The rope was put around the lead-horse's neck and other rawhide ropes were placed around the other horses' necks and attached to the packs. In this manner the single file of horses and their burdens crossed the Arroyo Hondo without mishap.

As is common in the Los Adais-Natchitoches area in the month of March, rains can come suddenly and frequently and this day was no exception. While the party was crossing the stream, a cold, peppering shower began which turned into a steady downpour. Immediately the two women began unpacking one of the horses. This pack contained several hides sewn together, the four corners were attached to four nearby grouped trees, a long pole was quickly cut and placed beneath this square of hides and a shelter was completed, the pole raising the center of the square about the four corners and causing the rain to run down the sides.

Meanwhile, Lagross and Jose had gathered firewood, being careful to split the branches to expose the dry inside halves of the wood. Soon a warm, drying fire was going. Jose whistled and El Trumpitero came to the shelter and Jose removed from the saddle bag two bottles of wine, some cheese and a loaf of brown, hard bread.

Guiterez spoke as he passed one bottle of the wine to the two women, For you Senora and Senorita, one bottle of the priests' wine, which is the reason I am here. I had gone to the Post Jean Baptiste des Natchitoches to get wine for the priests, Father Certa and Father Balligo. The bread from the good miller, Sieur Le Renaudiere, baked by Jacques Turpeaux, was sold to me by the good Doctor Bonnafons at Sieur Barme's

Store; I bought the cheese, which was brought to Nachitoches by Joseph Lattier, from the two Barberousses who have a trading post among the Yatasse Indians at El Campti. It is wonderful the Lord has granted man the power to prepare food in such a way that it is preserved for future consumption, here we sit on the Arroyo Hondo and enjoy a meal just as if we were sitting in our own homes."

While they were eating Guiterez had become conscious of the beauty of Francine Manuella. She seemed to have inherited all the beauty of both the Indian and French races. Here thought Jose is the woman for me, this one I intend to make my wife. Jose thought of the dowry and wondered if Lagross had provided such for his daughter. He knew this young maiden would be the ideal helpmate in his future business because she could speak French, Spanish and the Caddo languages.

Jose decided that he would make his intentions known to Lagross. Both the Lagross and Guiterez families had known each other for many years, and he felt that there was at least a bond of more than business, so he decided to ask Lagross' assistance in obtaining this land east of the Arroyo Hondo. He began explaining his idea to the French trader about building a kind of trading post, and eating place which would have accommodations to sleep weary travelers. Lagross liked the young Spaniard's idea and told him so, but, said Lagross, "one would need a wife to make such a venture complete." At this Jose made his intentions toward the trader's daughter clear by stating that he wished perhaps that he might have permission to pay court to his daughter. Lagross did not seem surprised of Guiterez' intentions, as many had asked for his daughter. "My daughter," said Lagross, "has had many suitors, some offered marriage and some only a proposition. You understand how some of the French and Spanish regard a half breed woman, however, those who offered a proposition now wear the mark of the short leather whip she always carries. As for my permission to pay court to my daughter, that is entirely up to her, she is certainly old enough to be married, according to other young women her age in this area. Many fathers of young girls are now pampering a grandchild. Francine is a very head-strong woman and it will take an unusual man to win her hand."

Meanwhile Francine, listening to this conversation, was amused, and first inclined to be angry, but then she thought, Jose offered marriage, not just a proposition as many had done. Guiterez cut quite a figure, either astride El Trumpitero or afoot, so this man might be just the one for her, but she wondered if his talk about the Three Cabins was not just so much talk.

"Jose Guiterez", said Francine, "Jose Guiterez, a *mestizo*, a half breed, wishes the hand of Francine Manuella Lagross, who is also a half breed; Guiterez who talks big and has nothing to offer a wife but an assumption of what he intends to do; my father who sits there agreeing with him while he drinks the Priests' wine and talks about me as though I were some sort of trade-goods; my mother sits there nodding her head in agreement, as if she would be glad to get rid of me; all of you talking as if I would have nothing to do with the situation. Do you think, Jose, that you can offer my father and mother wine, bread and cheese, that would be sufficient to win me as a wife? I notice that El Trumpitero does not have a whip mark on his hide, that the bit in his mouth is not the cruel Spanish bit used by the dragoons; you do not have the sharp Spanish spurs on your boots, do you think you can bend me to your will as you have El Trumpitero?" "Ha," she laughed, "that would be something to see. Now, mestizo, I have a proposition. The moon will be full tonight. If on the third full moon from this one, there are three cabins here on the Arroyo Hondo, then I will be your wife. If not I will have El Trumpitero, the horse I will ride when I leave here, you can use mine. You see, I know you have no money, no land to sell and no possible way to stock such a building with trade-goods and in the meantime you will not have El Trumpitero which is the only thing of value you do have; now Senor Jose Guiterez what do you say to that?"

"Well," said Guiterez, "for so small a woman you certainly have a large mouth, but first I must do this." He quickly grabbed Francine and put her across his knee as one would do a spoiled child and spanked her soundly. "First," he said, "for talking so to her parents and second, that she should show more respect to the man she is going to marry; third, he was holding her to her proposition; fourth, that if, when she was released, she struck him with her whip, he would use the whip on her so thoroughly that she would not be able to sit down for the three moons which she had previously mentioned." Lagross roared with laughter as his squaw whispered to him that Francine had finally met her match.

The rain had ceased and the group headed for Natchitoches, Francine astride El Trumpitero and Guiterez astride the horse of Francine. Not much was said until the train had reached the top of the steep hill called Grand Montania. Jose remarked that the horse of Francine had probably had the same temperament as her owner and she undoubtedly bit and kicked. Francine, not without a retort, stated that M. St. Denis could not grant land to a Spaniard, he would be a fool if he did, El Trumpitero was as good as hers right now. Guiterez said he had one thing that Francine had overlooked when she stated her proposition and that she was as good as married to him right now. So the two passed the time on the way to Natchitoches arguing with each other.

At Natchitoches Guiterez went to Sieur Barme's Store and obtained more wine for the priests at Los Adaìs. He then went to see St. Denis and told him of the occurrences of the day, and his intentions. St. Denis said, "I have no authority to do this other than to a Frenchman." "Now," said Madame St. Denis, who had evidently been eavesdropping on the conversation, "since when has M. De St. Denis ever questioned the word 'authority', especially in such a matter advantageous to the French as well as the Spanish, not to mention the extra profits in commissions to be received from trade goods sold Guiterez at this prospective trading post." "Madame," said St. Denis, "you underestimate me. I merely stated that I did not have the authority, I did not say that I would see that Guiterez did not get the land. Now go quickly and send someone to fetch Sieur Barme." When Sieur Barme arrived St. Dennis explained all to him. "Now", said St. Denis to Barme, "I will sell to you 10 arpents of land at the base of Grand Montania this side of the

Arroyo Hondo for ten percent of the first year's profits of the first year that this new trading post is in operation. I will sell this land to you in the name of the King of France, what you do with this land is your business. Now, Senor Guiterez wishes to buy some land, on this land he intends to build a trading post called The Three Cabins. If you wish to sell this land to Senor Guiterez for ten percent of the profits of his first year's business, you would be in accord with the law to do so. As far as merchandise for this said trading post I am sure your store could supply the necessary merchandise. As for payment, I am sure Senor Guiterez can be trusted, and as for security there would be the dowry given by Jean Lagross. If you are in agreement I will send for the Notary and draw up the papers. In the meantime you can issue a bill of sale to Senor Guiterez for the land." Addressing Guiterez, "Senor, you now own 10 arpents of land, but building the three cabins in the allotted time will take some doing. In the meantime you have many friends here at Natchitoches and I will see that they know about your problem."

Back at Los Adais Guiterez obtained an interview with the Governor, Winthuisin, to ask for permission to establish the Three Cabins on the French side of the Arroyo Hondo. The Governor at Los Adais agreed to Guiterez' request. Almazon had settled the question that the Arroyo Hondo was the boundary between the territories of France and Spain, and any Governor could give away land which did not belond to his country. Guiterez now had the sanction of both the French and the Spanish. When he explained all the details to his family and his many Spanish friends, all turned to with willing hands and the wilderness of the Arroyo Hondo rang with the echoes of many axes. Indians and Frenchmen from Natchitoches brought food and extra assistance. In less than the first moon two of the cabins were completed. Guiterez had Father Certa at Los Adais begin reading the banns for matrimony, and on the fourth Sunday Francine came down the steep trail of Grand Montania and looked at The Three Cabins finished and stocked with trade goods.

As the two left The Three Cabins to go to Los Adais to be

wed, Guiterez said to Francine, "Remember when you are estimating my values, I told you I had one thing that you had forgotten to name, that one thing was friends." "So you have", said Francine, "but did you not wonder where so much food came from to feed those who were building the three cabins, I am not without friends", and she smiled, "so, my high and mighty Guiterez, I think we are going to make a good match. Many of our friends think so too. Doesn't the female bird always help her mate build the nest? Look behind you at all those people coming to our wedding, they are your friends as well as mine". Guiterez gazed at Francine admiringly and said, "there is a blessing in rain in more ways than one."

IX

AFTER ST. DENIS

In 1743 Justo Bonev Y Morales was sent to replace Winthuisin as Governor. Morales, a Knight of the Order of Santiago, was a man befitting the ideals of St. Denis, who was now a Knight of the Order of St. Louis. These two visited often, two knights on a tiny western frontier. By now the French and Spanish had intermarried frequently so that the Arroyo Hondo barrier stood in name only.

On June 11, 1744, St. Denis died. Morales came to offer his condolences as did many from Los Adais. Indians and slaves alike bowed their heads to the memory of this man.

Governor Morales, in keeping with the false cold front of diplomacy, wrote his superiors, "St. Denis is dead, thank God, now we can breathe easier".

Captain Caesar de Blanc, a son-in-law of St. Denis, was appointed Post Commandante at Natchitoches and in the same year, 1744, Governor Morales was replaced by Francois Garcia Larios. These two men had no outstanding quarrels, for during these four years both the French and the Spanish prospered, crops were favorable and the trail from Los Adais was traveled daily by each of the nationalities. The Natchitoches area was prosperous and shipped to New Orleans, tobacco, cattle, horses and other farm products. Even those farmers at Los Adais were selling to the New Orleans market. Young Gil Y. Barbo was importing wild cattle and horses, obtained from the plains of Texas, driven over El Camino Real to the Adais-Natchitoches frontier, and on to New Orleans.

There was a working agreement between Juan de Mora and Lt. Derbonne, now retired from the French army and a civilian, farmer, trader and exporter of note in the Natchitoches post area.

In 1748 Pedro del Barrios Jacinto y Esprilla, an Alcolade of the Santo Hernando of all New Spain, was appointed the new Governor of Los Adais. The humdrum life of the frontier was too much for the new Governor so he gave up his position to Jacinto de Barrios y Gauregui in 1750. Barrios remained as governor until 1759, having had the fortitude to be Governor of Los Adais for a longer span of time than any of his predecessors. By now third generation Spaniards were being born on the Texas frontier from San Antonio De Bexar to Los Adais. These people were experiencing a new freedom not felt anywhere else in New Spain. They now regarded this land of Texas as their own. The seat of government was too far away to exercise a cloistered, ruling hand over them.

In 1759 Angle de Martos y Navarette replaced Jacinto Barrios as Governor of Los Adais. Navarette was a merchant and began to liven the frontier. Up to this time the French were supplying the area with all needed material, but when the new Governor came, fine Spanish lace, woolens and linen, finer than any which had previously been offered for sale on the frontier, and nails, which had always been scarce on the frontier, became plentiful.

In 1762 Louis XV gave Louisiana to his cousin Charles III of Spain.

In 1762 Caesar De Blanc was replaced at Natchitoches by Adrian Francois Le Doux as Post Commandante. He was in turn replaced by Angelus La Perrier in 1764. Perrier was the Commandante who received the first Catholic nuns to arrive in Natchitoches; thus 1765 marked the date of the beginning of formal scholastic training in the area.

Through his merchandising endeavors on this French-Spanish frontier Navarette had amassed for himself an estimated eighty thousand dollar fortune. In 1767 Don Hugo O'Connor was appointed Governor of the Adais and Texas coun-

try, and in November of that year, on the seventh day, Commandante La Perrier had the sad responsibility of turning over the
Natchitoches Post to Don Antonio Ulloa representing the
Spanish Government. In this same year O'Connor received a
visitor, Padre Jose de Solice, who kept a diary of his visitation
which was translated by Reverend Peter T. Forristal and was
published as one of the preliminary studies of the Texas-Coahuila
Historical Society.

Father Solice records the work of the priests of the Mission
de Los Adais. There were 256 baptisms, 64 marriages and 116
burials. At the Natchitoches Post he found records of 20 baptisms, 13 marriages and 15 burials. (Natchitoches was quite
often without the services of a priest and the padres of Los Adais
supplied their spiritual needs).

Also, in 1767 Athanase De Mezieres, a Frenchman, was
appointed Commandante of Post St. Jean Baptiste Des Natchitoches.

In 1770 Baron de Ripperda was appointed Governor of Los
Adais and it befell his duty to see to the evacuation of Presidio
Senors del Pilar de Los Adais. The Spanish authorities decided
that now that the Louisiana Territory was entirely under Spanish jurisdiction, this presidio was no longer necessary.*

Ripperda issued orders that all settlers and army personnel
were to be ready in three days to leave the area. Many of the
farmers fled to the Natchitoches area with their families and
worldly goods.

With Natchitoches now the seat of Government of the Texas
area westward to San Antonio, El Camino Real was lengthened
at least fifteen miles in extent from Natchitoches to Mexico
City. De Mezieres had under his jurisdiction an area extending
from Post Du Rapides (Alexandria) to the Ataquapois in Oklahoma southward to San Antonio.

---

*This Spanish Fort had stood for 48 years amid what was considered
a hostile area, yet in all that time it never had to defend itself. This belies
the statements or propaganda of the French referring to the cruelties and
unjust rule of the Spanish against the Indians of the area. Had such been
so, certainly the Indians would have risen in open rebellion.

The inhabitants of Los Adais and those residing around the missions in the Nacogdoches area were rebellious and Baron Ripperda extended his ultimatum to five days.

Antonio Gil y Barbo and Gil Flores became the heroes of the evacuation of Los Adais, some five hundred men, women and children moved to the vicinity of San Antonio. The former inhabitants of El Camino Real were not happy. They longed for the fertile soil and forests which abounded in wild game of the East Texas and West Louisiana area. Flores and y Barbo were sent with a petition to the Viceroy of Mexico. The two returned with the news that the people would be allowed to settle in a new area. They moved to a settlement on the Trinity River at Robbins Crossing, the present day location in Madison County, Texas.

Floods and the danger of hostile Indians soon forced the settlers to seek a new environment. They moved eastward to Nacogdoches under the leadership of y Barbo. There in 1779 was established the Town of Nacogdoches.

Y Barbo and a party of followers went back to Los Adais and dug up four of the six cannon buried there just prior to the evacuation of the area. They returned to Nacogdoches and re-established La Presidio de Neustra Senora de Los Delores de Nacogdoches and in the same year Antonio Gil y Barbo was appointed Commandante of the Presidio.

At Natchitoches in 1773 Commandante De Mezieres kept contact with all of this vast area by assigning traders to establish trading posts among the different Indian tribes and suppliers were assigned to each trader:

Pierre Bison was sent to the Calcasieu Indians, the supplier was Reme Poissot;

Louis Pablo Villeneuvf De Blanc to Caddoquopois, Bisadore was to supply him;

Jose Antonio Bonetis was sent to Atachapois, this man was an independent trader;

Pierre Blot was sent to the Nacogdoches Indians and Joseph Blancpain was to supply him;

Ceasar Barme was sent to the Yatasses near Campti, Louisiana;

Nicholas Chef was an independent trader to the Tokawanes; these were in an area fifty miles northwest of the present-day city of Fort Worth, Texas. It was one of the most remote trading posts from Natchitoches and De Mezieres assigned a supply-patrol of the militia at the Natchitoches Post to supply the necessary trade goods. Sergeant Joseph Trichell, who had been assigned to the Natchitoches Post in 1749, was to command the patrol which consisted of Corporal Nicholas Tournier and an accountant, Nicholas Le Noir. Four musketeers, Francois Hugue, Louis Moinet, Nicholas Pent and Andries Compiere. Domingo De Soto was to act as interpreter.

This patrol was responsible for the arrest of four Englishmen who had crossed the Mississippi River and were trading among the Tokawanes. The four men were William Warden, John Cross, John Hamilton and Jerome Matalinche.

De Mezieres was vexed with Sgt. Trichell for allowing the Englishmen to sell all of their trade goods to the Indians and threatened him with imprisonment, but Trichell explained that the Indians would have gone on the war path if they had not been allowed to trade for the English merchandise. Trichell countered with the fact that all of the profits of the English traders were now in his hands and that there was no difference if De Mezieres had the trade-goods or the profits. De Mezieres paid the Englishmen in French and Spanish coin equal to the original cost of the merchandise, and this same patrol was ordered to escort the Englishmen fifty miles east of Natchez before setting them free. The Englishmen were charged with the Patrol's expenses.

Luis de Quindise was an independent Spanish trader and was sent to the Adais Indians.

Pierre Dupain was sent to the Peticaddo;
Andre D'Hutrive was sent to the Bidias on the Trinity River;

Alexis Grappe was sent to the Ais and Guierlero Lestage was to supply him.

In 1770 DeMezieres following St. Denis' method of keeping peace with the Indians, invited the Chiefs to come and stand before him at Post Du Natchitoches to receive presents in the name of the King of Spain. Along El Camino Real traveled such great Chiefs as:

Tinhioune, Chief of the Caddoquopois.

Santo, head Chief of the Bidias and Don Melchor, otherwise called Gorgorritos, a sub Chief of the Bidias.

Quirotaches, Chief of the Nacogdoches Indians.

Christobal, Chief of the Taouaizes.

Vigotos, head Chief of the Hasinai Federation of Indians.

Thus, by gaining the friendship and allegiance of the most important Indian Chiefs of the territory, DeMezieres established an easy feeling between the Indians and the Spanish Government.

As of February 16, 1776 DeMezieres sent this Census Report to Unzaga, Governor at New Orleans:

113 homes; 105 heads of families with 86 women; 77 youths able to bear arms; 106 infants; 34 unmarried women; 84 bachelors and non residents engaged in hunting and fishing and trade with the Indians; 2 male and 2 female free people of color; 2 male and 1 female mulattos; 410 Indian and negro slaves (men. women and children) ; 277 pieces of fire arms; 1258 head horses, 842 head cattle, 3000 head sheep and goats and 783 hogs and 481 mules. There was shipped from Natchitoches: 1000 head horses; 100 mules; 9 quintals of indigo; 15 fenegas of indigo seed; 30,000 packages of tobacco; 120 buffalo hides; 36,000 deer hides; 5000 ambrias of bear oil; 5000 pounds of tallow, quantities of bacon and meats, both salted and dried.

X

AFTER THE LOUISIANA PURCHASE

In 1802 Louisiana was ceded back to France by Spain by the Treaty of Ildefonso. On May 2, 1803 Livingston and Monroe signed with Barbe-Marbois the purchase treaty which was dated back to April 30, 1803; thus Louisiana became a possession of the United States.

Spain did not approve of the sale of Louisiana and decided to reclaim all of the land originally occupied prior to the time when Louisiana was ceded to Spain.

There was a movement of Spanish soldiers under the command of General Hurrera as far as Nacogdoches and from there patrols were sent across the Sabine River.

Fort Claiborne, established in 1805 at Natchitoches by orders of General Wilkinson, was occupied by several companies of the Second Infantry of the United States Army under the command of Major Porter.

Dr. John Sibley had been appointed Indian Agent for this area of the Soutwestern Frontier by Governor Claiborne. Dr. Sibley had been keeping an account of the Spanish patrol movements east of the Sabine River through contact with the Indians of the area. On February 2, 1806, he sent a letter to Major Moses Porter at Fort Claiborne saying that there was a detachment of Spanish militia encamped at Juan Mora's Lagoon, also known as Conichi Ranch, one league east of Los Adais on Bayou Dupont.

Lt. Piatt was sent with a letter to Nacogdoches, demanding

that all Spanish patrols east of the Sabine River retire immediately to the west bank of that stream.

Captain Edward D. Turner left for the Los Adais area with a detachment of soldiers on February 5, 1806. The Spanish patrol was contacted and Captain Turner delivered the ultimatum of Major Porter that it retire to the west bank of the Sabine River*

This document from the U. S. Army records shows the result of that meeting: The beginning of the Neutral Strip.

At the Adais

February 6, 1806.

I, Joseph Maria Gonzalez, commandante of his most Catholic Majesty's troops on this side of the Rio Sabinas, hereby having agreed with Captain Edward D. Turner, Captain in the United States Army, to return all troops of his Catholic Majesty's to the other side of the said Rio Sabinas, as soon as my horses will permit it or in five days, or at the most six, and to make my march this day and I also oblige myself to not send any more patrols on this side of the Rio Sabinas.

Signed: Ensign Joseph Maria Gonzalez

Witness: John V. Duforest (Interpreter)

The above document was the result of an agreement establishing a no-man's land between the Arroyo Hondo and the Sabine River, which neither the United States Government nor the Mexican Government would use, until a final settlement could be reached between the two said governments about a boundary. This agreement was made by two young officers representing their respective countries, both willing to fight for their countries, but both having the intelligence and initiative to declare a stalemate to prevent a war.

---

*At this point one must understand the claims of the United States concerning the Louisiana Purchase. The United States claimed the Rio Grande as the boundary of the land previously owned by France because of La Salle's settlement at Fort Louis on Matagordo Bay in 1685. The Spanish claimed the land as far as the west bank of the Red River, basing their claim on the Domingo Teran del Rios' expedition of 1690. Both the Spanish and the United States' officers involved in the meeting in the Adais area were aware of the claims of their respective countries.

This forty mile wide strip of land became known as the Neutral Strip, and in it gathered the lawless of both countries. Even so, from within this lawless area were to come men who would strike the first blow for Texas independence.

In 1807 several slaves of Louis Derbonne and other planters owning land adjoining the Neutral Strip, fled into the Neutral Strip and from there they went to Nacogdoches and on to Trinidad de Salcedo on the Trinity River, where they were given refuge by the Spanish Government.

On September 5, 1807, Don Manuel de Salcedo, Governor of Texas at Nacogdoches, received a letter saying:

> The planters of the Natchitoches area are threatening to organize a force of 250 men to go after slaves known to be in the Texas area of Nacogdoches and at Trinidad de Salcado unless the slaves are returned.

The letter reminded the Spanish Governor of Article XX of the treaty between the United States and Mexico which said fugitive slaves must be returned to their owners. The letter was signed by Judge John Carr, and Justices Rouquier and Paillette.

The above letter and a letter from Governor Claiborne brought about the desired results. The governor might have been influenced by the knowledge of the Phillip Nolan filibustering expedition in 1800 which spent itself at Waco-Texas vicinity. Nolan had for several years traveled westward from the Alexandria, Louisiana area and established a trail straight westward into the Texas-San Antonio area, where he was trading for and capturing wild horses and cattle. This trail later became known as Nolan's Trace

XI

THE DEVIL'S PLAY GROUND

When Generals Wilkinson and Herrera agreed to the boundaries set by their two junior officers, Turner and Gonzalez, they created a back door to the United States of a forty-mile-wide strip which was to become one of the most lawless places that ever existed within the confines of the United States.

Every outlaw and murderer made this Neutral Strip his destination, The Free State of Sabine, it was called. Neither Spain nor the United States wished to have the responsibility or the expense of policing this outlaw state, although the southland's busiest road cut through the center of it. But traffic was heavy just the same. Many found that the only safe way to cross the strip was to travel in force, therefore, either at Natchitoches or on the west side of Sabine River, the travelers waited until a large enough group was gathered to guarantee safe travel.

The outlaws of the Strip dealt in horse stealing, cattle rustling, counterfeiting, or any other form of crime that might strike their fancy. There is no definite data or history of the goings-on inside the area, but many men who lived in, or traveled through the district recorded their experiences in diaries and stories or just handed down hearsay tales of the happenings in this lawless land. There, a person's security was strapped at his hips or carried in his hands in the form of pistols, long rifles or knives. Even the long, rawhide whip was considered a deadly weapon in the hands of an expert.

Los Adais was a waystation and on the bulletin board appeared one day a word with a new meaning, *Sabina 28*, the same sign appeared on the Rendezvous Oak at Natchitoches. To the average citizen it meant nothing, but to those in the know it meant slaves would be for sale at a point near Pendleton at the ferry on Sabine River on the 28th of that month.

With the discovery of a new way to granulate sugar and with the invention of the cotton gin, the land around Los Adais and Natchitoches became highly productive when planted in sugar cane and cotton and more slaves were needed, but the United States had forbidden their importation.

To Jean Lafitte, the pirate, the Sabine River with the protection of the Neutral Strip, became the back door to the United States. Slaves for wagon loads of food were commonly exchanged, according to the statements of a Mr. Tulley at Los Adais and Mr. Gunlineau at Natchitoches. Lafitte needed food for his pirate operations. Up the Sabine River the boats were pulled, poled or paddled by the slaves to be sold. From the Los Adais and Natchitoches areas came wagon loads of food, smoked hams, kegs of salted bacon, cornmeal, kegs of molasses, wine, corn whiskey, dried beans, peppers, tobacco, sweet potatoes and gourds of honey, with spiced cake sent by hopeful wives to the pirates so that their husbands might make more profitable deals.

Back on the same wagons came the slaves, bolts of cloth, jewelry and perfume (Lafitte's storehouses was filled with goods from every Spanish and British ship that he could capture). Everything was legal as far as the bills of sale went. A certain honest merchant in New Orleans, with a good reputation and scruples, signed blank bills of sale, to be filled in by Tulley and Gunlineau.

This may seem rather crude to the average reader—the smuggling of slaves and the ladies sending spiced goods to the pirates on the Sabine River. At this very time the United States was confiscating where it could slaves that had been smuggled in, selling them and giving the informers half of the proceeds of the sales. Nothing was said about putting the slaves on a boat and returning them to their homeland (Question: Are there very many people today who try to beat the Income Tax?) There was some good to come out of all this. Lafitte assisted the United States in the defense of New Orleans in the war of 1812, furnishing men, ammunition and food. Where did he obtain the food? From the Los Adais and Natchitoches area. Lafitte, Tulley and Gunlineau were merely supplying the demand for a necessary merchandise and certainly the slaves were better off because of it.

Noah Smithwick, who had visited the Strip, wrote of the murders, robberies and numerous violations of law there. He gives us one tale that falls in line with the demand and supply of the times. Because the man he wrote about was still alive he calls this character, John Doe. Doe was a counterfeiter of money, especially the Mexican silver dollar. The people at that time had no "jingling" money for their pockets and Doe supplied this demand, with a silver-coated copper coin. Because of a slight flaw in the press the coins were easily identified and called Doe's dollars,

An Indian approached Doe one day and handed him one of the counterfeit dollars requesting that Doe put a new skin on it. Doe obliged by giving the Indian a new counterfeit dollar for the old one, explaining to the Indian that dollars were like snakes, they always shed their skins. Doe's dollars, although not recognized outside the Strip, were regarded as legal tender therein.

It was said that Doe's dollars were of more handsome design than the original Mexican Eagle Silver Dollar.

Doe, however, minted pure silver dollars of the same design. He mixed enough of these with the bogus dollars so that on occasion when a dollar was questioned and the dollar tested, it was found to be of pure silver.

Doe, like all counterfeiters, wished to extend his operations but he wandered out of the Strip on the American side and was arrested.

Every old place has its ghost story and "Spanish Town" is no exception:

A young Spaniard had successfully traveled the Strip, bringing with him wealth and many fine cloths. He settled at Spanish Town and became the target of every single maiden

— 85 —

ARKANSAS

TEXAS

LOUISIANA

Shreveport

Coushatti

RED

Campti.

Natchitoches.

San Augustine

Robeline

RIVER

Montgomery.

EL CAMINO REAL

Nacogdoches.

Pendleton Ferry.

NOLANS TRACE

Colfax.

Alexandria.

NECHES RIVER

SABINE RIVER

CALCASIEU RIVER

Sabine Lake
a Pirate
Rendevous.

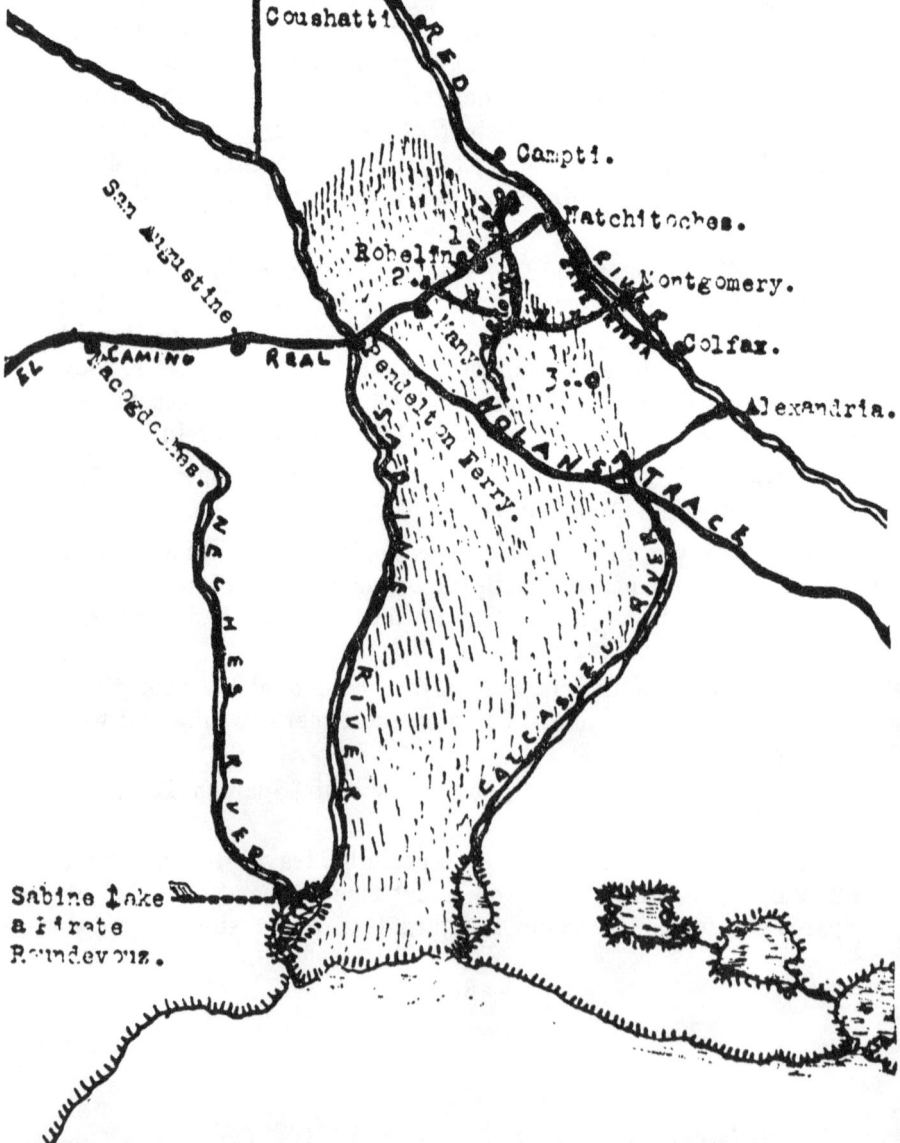

there. Mariea Guiterriz, who had many suitors, won his heart. Anyone attempting to pay court to her ran the risk of losing his life in a duel with other jealous suitors. Immediately after the wedding at the reception a disappointed lover insulted the groom. Swords flashed, Mariea rushed between the duelists, a sword stabbed her—not a serious wound all were assured but infection set in and she grew worse. An old Indian gave some herbs to the young Spaniard with instructions how to use them to stop the infection. "Boil these herbs together over a small fire, the odor of the brew will change and when the odor is this", the Indian allowed the Spaniard to smell the brew, "remember the odor because now will be the time to soak the poultice with the solution", then the Indian was gone.

The young husband followed the instructions and Mariea began to improve, but the herbs ran out and the Indian could not be found. Mariea sickened again. The Spaniard went to the creek banks and the marshy places searching for the herbs, building countless tiny fires, brewing grasses and leaves, trying to re-discover the combination of herbs that would produce the exact odor he was seeking.

OPPOSITE PAGE

THE NEUTRAL STRIP
(shaded area shown)

1. Spanish Town and Scuffelville.
2. Half-way-house or Twenty-mile-house, near Many, La.
3. Kisatchie Caves, near Kisatchie, Louisiana.

xxxx. The Sabine Trail, from Montgomery to the Half-way-house near Many. The Planters on Red and Cane Rivers used this road when going to the Sabine River to trade for Slaves.

Nolan's Trace, cut across the southern part of the Strip from Point Coupee, Phillip Nolan blazed this Trail and used it to trade for horses in the Texas area.

This Lawless Strip of land lasted from 1806 to 1821. It was often referred to as "The Free State of Sabine".

Note:

I show Cane River on this map, However at the time of the beginning of the Strip, Cane River was Red River. I show Red River as it is today, to show the locations of the Towns, whose People were involved in trade in the Neutral Strip.

By the year 1821, the Red River had begun to change its course to the Rigolett de Bon Duex, which was a Bayou extending from a point just above Natchitoches to Colfax, La. Thus you see the Actual water ways as they are today. (Drawn by the author)

Mariea's infection worsened and she died. The young man's mind, not able to grasp the reality that his love had gone, became affected. His brain ceased to function past the last day that he had left her, assuring her that this would be the day that he would discover the correct blend of the herbs. From that time on, fires, tiny fires could be seen on the creek banks in the swamps and on the hillsides—a lover, true and devoted, still seeking the odor that would save the life of his beloved wife.

The crazy Spaniard, they called him, and those who came in contact with him, those who knew the details of his sad story, made the Sign of the Cross when he passed and silently said a prayer for him.

Night and day he searched for the elusive odor, always searching. Those of his age, grew old and died, and so did their sons and grandsons, but the legend lived on.

Some say they can still see him in his never-ending search, smartly dressed as he kneels by a tiny fire, others say he is old, dirty, ragged and ugly; but all say there is no need to be alarmed because this ghost walks with God.

If some day or night you see a tiny fire with a shadow kneeling by it, then you, too, are walking with God, because you, too, are one possessed of devotion and love.

XII

SATAN'S AGENT — JOHN A. MURRELL

One of the many buried treasures of the Sabine strip is claimed to belong to John A. Murrell, who possessed a brilliant mind which he used to break all the Commandments that God gave Mosses on Mount Sinai. He was the type of man who could recite to another the entire books of the Old and New Testaments then shoot him down in cold blood.

John A Murrell was born about the year 1800 in Williams County, Tennessee. His father was a Methodist Minister and his mother, a mountain woman, who at that time operated a wayside tavern. Through the teachings of his father he learned the Gospel and through the teachings of his mother he learned to steal. Murrell, well equipped with the knowledge of the good and the bad often passed as a preacher. In this guise he made his appearance in the Neutral Strip.

About the year 1825 Murrell went about preaching the Gospel and at the same time was organizing a band of outlaws. At Los Adais which was now called Spanish Town, at Twenty Mile House or Midway Station near Fort Jesup, in the hidden caves near Kisatchie, he established his headquarters and from these places he ranged out of the Strip to preach to the more populated communities.

Murrell could mimic the voices of many people and was an excellent actor. In each community where he preached he adapted their tone of voice and mannerisms. One of his favorite gospels was the one he called "Directions". As he addressed his audience he may have been standing in the pulpit of a church, or atop a stump or standing in the bed of a wagon, wherever a crowd gathered Murrell felt that he should preach to them.

"Directions," he would shout, "always when one begins a journey, he has a destination. The road to this destination is similar to the Road of Life, often along this road one has to inquire about directions, and it is so through the Journey of Life, one must follow directions laid down by the Church and the Ministers, they are the sign posts that point the way. Quite often a man while traveling this road, decides to take a short cut, instead of following the Good Book as laid down by the Church, these short cuts become his mis-deeds or his sins.

We shall assume that this Bible is the Book of Judgment and in it will be the names of every living person on the face of the earth. By each name there are two columns, one for his assets or his good deeds of life and the other column for his mis-deeds, which we shall call his de-sets,"

From here on Murrell becomes the actor in what he called, The Drama at the Gates of Heaven.

"Batiste had made the journey through life and was knocking on the Gates of Heaven, a voice from within asks, who knocks? Batiste answers and gives his full name. The voice is that of St. Peter who looks up Batiste's record of life in the Book of Judgment. Then St. Peter explains to Batiste, we take out the pages which contain your assets and place them on one side of the scales of justice and on the other side we place the pages of your de-sets. If your assets out-weigh your de-sets, then naturally you can come in, as we place your assets and de-sets upon the scales we will review them."

(Now Murrell becomes the comic for the benefit of his audience). "Right here Batiste on May 25, you done de-setted enough to carry over on the next three pages. Boy, you was really de-setting that day.

Here, we see your Pastor found you hunting on Sunday and you had a nice bag of squirrels, the Pastor spoke to you about it and you gave the excuse that you had your days mixed up. Again he caught you fishing on Sunday and a nice bunch you had too, you gave the excuse that you had your days mixed up again.

Now, if you had given the Pastor some of those squirrels or fish, then those de-sets of that day would have turned into assets. But all along the Road of Life you gave the excuse that you had your days mixed up. 'Now,' said St. Peter, as he looked at the scales, 'because you had your days mixed up you now have your directions mixed up. You all done come the wrong way', and he shut the door in Batiste's face. Batiste begged for another chance but this could not be, as you know you can only travel the Road of Life once."

Along the Neutral Strip the inhabitants catered only to hard money, that is gold and silver coins, and Murrell asked that fees for his service be paid in coin.

Murrell would place a set of balancing scales where everyone could see, on one side he placed the Bible, then he said, "this Bible will represent the Book of Judgment and I place it on this side of the scales, it will represent your mis-deeds or de-sets. Now, we are all going to stay here until you people give enough to tip these scales to the asset side." While the collections were being made, Murrell would be expounding of the good things he intended doing with the money, he even had a few henchmen in the audience to begin the contributions and to urge the others to do the same.

Murrell becomes another legend of Los Adais and of his hidden treasures, it is believed that he had many hidden treasures which he called large banks and small banks.

No one is certain how Murrell's death came about. Murrell's gold and silver, and he must have had much of it, with nearly a decade of preaching, lying, robbing and murdering in the strip, could have been the cause.

XIII

THE BREAK-UP OF THE NEUTRAL STRIP

There were rumors in 1806 that Aaron Burr was attempting to organize the settlers of the Neutral Strip and that an actual Free State of Sabine was to be established, Breastworks at Sabine-Town and a Block House with two companies of the United States militia were established near the confluence of Bayou Negrett and the Sabine River on the El Camino Real.

The establishment of the Block House by General Wilkinson resulted in the Spanish bolstering their strength in the western part of the Neutral Strip by giving presents to the Indians and thereby establishing an Indian barrier in the area.

The gifts amounted to two thousand seven hundred-nine pesos from the Mexican Government to be given at Nacogdoches. The Indians received muskets, lead, powder, shot, knives, razors, scissors, combs, mirrors, glass beads, war paint, copper and iron pots, ribbons, coats, bells, needles, belt buckles, ramrods, cotton goods and rum. The Indians asked for tobacco which was not available, but five hundred eighty-nine pounds of tobacco twists were smuggled from Natchitoches through the Neutral Strip to Nacogdoches by orders of Manuel de Salcedo, the Governor. Although trade was forbidden on El Camino Real by the Spanish from French Louisiana there was a continuous stream of contraband goods being smuggled into Texas. The "Contraband Trail" ran parallel to the El Camino Real about four miles distant from the El Camino Real, but crossing it intermittently in areas that were uninhabited.

The Americans retaliated by supplying the Takuays and the Towanoni with articles of trade and a blacksmith shop so they could sharpen the knives and scissors obtained as presents from the Spanish.

Outlaws left the Neutral Strip to raid isolated farms and plantations. Slave stealing and cattle rustling were not overlooked. The citizens complained to the United States Government.

Lieutenant Augustus McGee and Lieutenant Zebulon M. Pike were ordered to disperse the bandits of the Neutral Strip. The orders of General Hampton expressed a desire for cooperation from the Spanish at Nacogdoches. A detachment under Captain Bernardino Mantero was sent from Nacogdoches to assist Captain W. H. Overton, who was at that time the senior officer at Fort Claiborne, issued orders for the clearance of the strip on March 5, 1812. The military only succeeded in destroying the hideouts which were occupied by the bandits by burning everything in sight. The bandits knew every sneak trail of the Neutral Strip and were successful in avoiding the policing parties.

By the year 1821 the Anglo-American Civilization had crossed in substantial numbers the Mississippi River in two main divisions, Louisiana and Missouri.

General Edmund Pendleton Gaines considered that the most vital and important area of the southwest was: "The Southern section of the Western Frontier, from the mouth of the Sabine River eastward to the Red River and thence to the Mexican boundary at a point where the western boundary intersects the Sabine River."

General Jackson had transferred General Gaines, at that time commanding the Florida frontier, to the western frontier in 1817. General Gaines was aware of the constant unrest of the so-called "neutral strip," known as "The Free State of Sabine" and *No Man's Land*.

The proclamation of the Treaty of Washington in 1821 fixed the western boundary of the United States as the Sabine River, thus the agreement with the Mexican Republic transferred the Neutral Strip to the United States.

General Gaines was aware of the feeling of those settlers from the Sabine River westward along El Camino Real to the

Rio Grande near Eagle Pass, Texas. These were Spaniards that had felt the freedom of being so far from their government's head in Mexico City. They, with the Anglo-American settlers, wanted a different kind of freedom, not allegiance to Mexico or to the United States. Thus, the Fort Jesup-Natchitoches and El Camino Real Area on the eastern end from Nacogdoches and San Augustine was ripe for the filibusterers.

There were many in this area, Gaines was certain, who did not recognize the Treaty of Washington, Frenchmen of the fifth and sixth generations who had settled this area, likewise the Spanish, and the Indians for countless generations before either of the other two nationalities.

"This land 'tis mine—'tis yours—'tis mine," said the French and the Spanish. "The land is mine," stated the United States, "we bought it from the French." The Indian declared, " 'tis mine, was so even before either the French or Spanish came." The settlers questioned which government will recognize our claim to the homesteads, the land grants, "this is mine by right of occupation."

There were the half-breeds, descendants of a French or Spanish father and an Indian woman. These were demanding their birthright. And they held sway over many Indian tribes. They were intelligent, they could be friendly, or a ruthless enemy. But the United States' ownership backed by the Army soon restored peace and order to No Man's Land.

XIV

THE FILIBUSTER OF 1812 - 1821

Don Jose Bernardo Maxmilliano Gutierrez de Lardo, often called Bernardo, was a merchant and blacksmith at Revilla, a village near the junction of the Rio Salado and the Rio Grande. He was a follower of Padres Miguel Hidalgo y Castillo and Jose Maria Morelos, who were encouraging a revolt among the Indian and Indian halfbreeds called *mestizos*.

Gutierrez with Captain Jose Manchaca, a Texas rebel and a deserter from the Royalist Army of Mexico, and ten others left Revilla with thirty thousand dollars in Mexican silver. Their objective was to reach Natchitoches, a border town on the Neutral Strip. The money was for organizing a filibuster campaign into Texas. They were pursued by the Royalists and were caught up with near the village of Bayou Pierre (a village at that time located on a road between the present-day Pleasant Hill and Lake End on Red River). Gutierrez and Manchaca escaped but lost the silver, finding refuge at a small trading post at Campti, Louisiana. When they arrived in Natchitoches and began recruiting men for the filibustering campaign they found many ready and willing to participate. The merchants, sensing enormous profits, offered every assistance.

Captain Manchaca went immediately into the Neutral Strip to solicit recruits among the bandits, or anyone else who desired to join the filibusterers.

Gutierrez wrote a letter to James Monroe, Secretary of State in Washington, explaining that although Texas was not yet a Republic the people of that area had all the necessary qualifications for becoming a nation, that it would be to the advantage of the United States and the people of the future Republic of Texas for them to seek assistance where they could find it. It would, therefore, be advantageous to the United States, should their undertaking be successful in overthrowing the yoke of the Mexican Government, and Texas become a Republic.

Gutierrez secured letters of recommendation and two hundred dollars from Dr. John Sibley and departed immediately for Washington where he met with officials and made requests for men, money, munitions and other supplies necessary for the filibustering campaign. Gutierrez brought out the importance to the United States of the Texas commerce. The proposal was dropped by the officials when Gutierrez insisted that he be in command of the expedition. However, Monroe did see the advantage of the United States having a Republic to the west to help guard the border, as at that time the United States was having difficulties with Spain and England, and because of the Florida question. Therefore the Secretary of State did offer encouragement to Gutierrez.

Don Jose Alvares de Toledo was at the same time in Washington seeking assistance for a revolution in Cuba, which if successful, would result in the establishment of an Antillean Confederation of the Islands. This, too, met with the approval of Monroe, but again he offered only encouragement and no assistance. Don Luis de Onis, the Minister from Spain, having learned of Toledo's plans, conspired with Diago Correga to do away with Toledo. Toledo, because of his failure to get the necessary assistance he desired, cast his lot with Gutierrez. He cultivated the friendship of General Ira A. Allen, who was looked upon with disfavor in the State of Vermont. Allen helped Toledo and Gutierrez by gaining the confidence and support of those who were interested in such an adventure, namely: Samuel Alden, a young adventurer; Aaron Mower, a printer by trade; Evariste Calvettes, a Frenchman of unusual but intriguing reputation, and William A. Prentis, a merchant who interested Henry Adams Bullard in the adventure of the filibuster campaign. This group of men, with several others departed for Natchitoches.

Gutierrez in Natchitoches had enlisted under his banner, the aid of Lieutenant August McGee, who resigned at Fort Claiborne to join the filibusterers; Samuel Kemper, a well-known figure in the politics of Florida; Rubin Ross, an ex-sheriff from Virginia; Henry Perry of the Army Quartermaster; Joseph B. Wilkinson, son of General James Wilkinson; J. McClanahan; Rubin Smith; James Patterson; A. Cole and Alexis Grappe, traders who had many contacts in Texas as far as San Antonio de Bexar; and James Gaines, brother of General Gaines. The merchants in Natchitoches hired some of the local youths, Tenoss Moinet, two Prudhommes, Henry Derbonne, Jose Benetis, Anthony Dubois, Peter Dolet, Michael Chesneau, Andrew Chase, Stephen Wallace, Matthew Bonnette, Walter Young, Joseph Ruth and Chesneau Tontin to go along to protect their interests and to bring back the contraband which they were sure would be obtained on such an expedition.

William Shaler arrived in Natchitoches almost on the heels of Gutierrez, a special agent sent by the Secretary of State Monroe to assist the new so called Gutierrez-McGee expedition. Shaler's letters to Monroe give an excellent account of the organization and execution of this expedition. Shaler, who had been trained as a military man, contributed greatly to its efficiency.

Samuel Davenport of the firm of Davenport and Barr, licensed traders, established themselves in the Soledad building in Nacogdoches. Davenport wrote to Don Manuel de Salcedo, Governor of Texas at Nacogdoches, from Natchitoches, "John Adair was gathering troops in Rapides (Alexandria, Louisiana) 500 men were being gathered along the Mississippi River and at Natchez. Captain Jose Manchac has gathered over a hundred men out of the Neutral Strip and they are now camped on the west bank of the Sabine River."

A letter was sent from Washington to the district judge notifying him that the United States would not sanction an organization of men on its land which would constitute an act of aggression against the government of another country. Judge Carr's answering letter dated July 22, 1812, stated that he was aware that some sort of movement of aggression was being talked about in the Natchitoches Area, but that to his knowledge there were no men grouped east of the Sabine River congregating with filibuster intent.

"Young men in groups of two, five, ten or fifteen arrive here in Natchitoches every day, many are from our immediate local area, they are mild-mannered and quiet and cause no disturbances, they purchase supplies at the local stores and when questioned about their destination, they declare that they are going on a hunting trip. I have no grounds with which I can detain such a small party of men, for to be sure groups fewer than fifteen or twenty cannot be classed as a filibustering party. If rumors are true and there is a location on the west bank of the Sabine River where men are gathering with the intent of invading Texas, that area is out of the jurisdiction of any one person representing our local or federal government."

On August 8, 1812, the campaign began with a total strength of one hundred eighty men.

At Nacogdoches was the proof that the people of the area, according to the statements of the traders Smith, Grappe, Patterson and McClanahan, were ready for a rebellion against the Spanish Government. At Nacogdoches on August 11, 1812, when the attack began, the filibusterers met only token resistance and one hundred ninety of the inhabitants joined the patriots. The easy fall of Nacogdoches was a shot in the arm for the filibusterers. Fifty of the Spanish soldiers joined with the rebels. A mule and horse train with booty of wool, hides and Spanish silverware, estimated to be valued at one hundred thousand dollars, was sent to Natchitoches to be exchanged for the necessary provisions to conduct the campaign. Henry Perry of the army quartermaster was there to receive the merchandise. Now he had something to work with. Supplies which could not be obtained in Natchitoches were purchased in Natchez, Mississippi. The merchandise was brought over the old Natchez-Vidalia to Natchitoches Indian trail (highway 84 today) which had its share of bandits and land-pirates.

Gutierrez was an old hand at spreading propapganda and at Nacogdoches the "rebels" paused long enough to make use of the talents of Aaron Hower, the printer. The news of the fall of Nacogdoches would be sure to bring volunteers from the Natchitoches-Neutral Strip area. On September 1, 1812, circulars were found as far as San Antonio, announcing that the filibusterers army had reached a thousand in number of well equipped men, and that more volunteers were arriving every hour from ten to one hundred in number to join Gutierrez, and that they now had cannon which had been taken from the Spanish in Nacogdoches.

Governor Salcedo, who had previously sent a message asking for assistance, received news that no help could be sent because the "Patriot Army" in Mexico was marching on Camargo and Nueva Santanadar (this was a group of rebel followers of Padres Castillo and Morelos). The propaganda news leaflets and the news from Mexico caused Salcedo to withdraw all outlying Spanish detachments and concentrate them at San Antonio de Bexar. At this stage of the campaign the McGee-Gutierrez army numbered no more than seven hundred men.

Now, Salcedo's military ability began to show. He needed a day or two so that the troops in the west under General Herrera could reach San Antonio. He left La Bahia (now Goliad, Texas) without defense and spread his troops along the Guadelupe River twenty-eight miles north and east of San Antonio. The filibusterers could not overlook the opportunity of taking a defenseless town. La Bahia fell without a struggle and the filibusterers were jubilant. Meanwhile the Spanish forces met, forming a total strength of nearly nine hundred men. Over fifty of the Spanish soldiers with the filibusterers deserted and returned to the Royalist troops, explaining they had been captured and were finally able to escape.

Up to now McGee had been in charge of the filibusterers and Gutierrez was the commander in name only. There was friction between McGee and Gutierrez, and at the same time Toledo was vying for the position of commanding them. Samuel Davenport, the unfaithful Indian Agent of Salcedo, who had joined the filibusterers, suddenly decided he had some important, unfinished business and departed for Nacogdoches. A day or so later Rubin Ross left to contact Indians encamped on the Sabine River with the intention of joining the filibusterers. McGee died at La Bahia under mysterious circumstances. Gutierrez claimed that McGee took poison to keep from being shot. Davenport stated that McGee was sick when he left for Nacogdoches, and Rubin Ross declared McGee was in good health two days prior to his leaving Davenport, and that at no time was he aware that McGee was sick.

When Ross contacted the Caddo Indians on the Sabine River Chief Tohois refused to fight under any flag other than that of the United States. Groups of the Alabamas, Choctaws, Conchattas and Attapaws on learning of the refusal of Tohois also refused to assist in the cause. However, nearly a hundred of the warriors did join with Rubin Ross.

The second attack of the Royalists was also a disappointment to Salcedo and the Spanish forces retired to San Antonio. On March 19, Ross returned with nearly two hundred Indian, Spanish and American volunteers and the march on San Antonio began. They met no opposition until they reached Rosillo, about eight miles from San Antonio; there, Samuel Kemper and Rubin Ross led a vicious charge and the main force of the rebel drive carried well into San Antonio.

The Spanish were defeated and surrendered unconditionally. Atrocities followed under the orders of Gutierrez who had declared himself President of the New Republic of Texas. Several of the Spanish officers were killed, their clothing stripped from their bodies and left exposed to the elments. The Americans were enraged by this action. After going to the scene of the atrocity and burying the dead, many followed the example of Warren D. C. Hall, deserted the filibusterers and left for their respective habitats.

A Junta was called after the arrival of Henry A. Bullard and James B. Wilkinson; Major James Perry and Captains Kemper and Ross threatened to leave with the Americans unless Gutierrez was ousted and Toledo named leader of the New Republic.*

The battle on the Madina River was the downfall of the filibusterers. The Spanish gathered their forces under the command of Colonels Joquine de Arrendondo y Miono and Ignacio Elizondo. After the battle the victors were lenient with the many Americans they had captured. Colonel Elinzondo issued a horse and rifle to each along with a passport for safe conduct back to the Sabine River. The Indians were included with the group freed, but with instructions to return to their tribes and never take up arms against the Spanish again.

It is interesting to note that many of these Americans were later successful in attempting to make the Texas area a Republic. On September 28, 1813, the first blow for Texas independence failed, but it had been proved, however, that the Spaniards north of the Rio Grande were influenced by the freedoms of the American traders along El Camino Real. They had been forced to provide for themselves from the fruits of the land, thus becoming independent in their own right. The easy fall of Nacogdoches was outstanding proof of their feelings.

---

*John Quincy Adams remarked of the Filibusterers: "The main actors cross and double-cross one another so frequently that suspicion and doubt hang over their hands like a black cloud over their actions."

RIVER

RED

RIVER

RIVER

CANE RIVER

RED RIVER

RED RIVER

NATCHITOCHES

FORT CLAIBORNE 1804

OLD RIVER

LA JEUNE

BAYOU

BAYOU PIERRE

RED RIVER

GRANDE ECORRE

RED

CAMP 1831
FORT SELDON 1821

AROYO HONDO

ROAD TO THE TEXAS

CANOE BAYOU

LITTLE RIVER

BAYOU PIERRE

CAMP 1831
RIO ADAIS

ROBELINE

SPANISH TOWN

ADAIS

CAMINO REAL

FORT JESUP DEFENSE AREA

BAYOU DUPONT

FORT JESUP 1822

SITE OF SABINE BLOCKHOUSE — 1807—TO 1834
AND CAMP SABINE — 1807—TO 1831

BAYOU NEGRET

TEXAS — ROAD — OR — EL CAMINO REAL

SABINE TOWN

SABINE RIVER

GAINES FERRY

XV

FORT JESUP

It seems odd that all that had happened in the nearly three hundred years preceding was merely a prelude to a settlement on a vital point, this one hill top in Sabine Parish.

The Caddo Nation of Indians was first to recognize the importance of this land extending from San Antonio to Natchitoches and settled it. What these Indians did not settle or cultivate they commercialized, and they established trade routes there.

Cabeza De Vaca and his companions came in 1530. They claimed no land but were searching for a way out.

Hernando De Soto in 1541 came, but by the time he had reached the Adais, he, too, was searching for a way out. He claimed no land.

Robert de La Salle came down the Mississippi River in 1682 and claimed all land drained by that River for the King of France. In the history of a country there is always one man who has the imagination to see its possibilities and the ability and push to realize his ambitions. Such a man was La Salle.

La Salle's second venture to the mouth of the Mississippi River resulted in failure. He came by sea, missed the mouth of the Mississippi River and settled on the coast of Texas where he later was killed. La Salle's expedition, however, aroused the Spanish of Mexico, who then began to extend their operations further to the north.

Padre Hidalgo's letter and St. Denis' answer resulted in the settlement of El Camino Real from San Antonio to Natchitoches.

Here then, was cast the first seed, in form of settlers, who learned to live as the Indians—free as the wind, this newly found freedom had been felt by settlers and their descendants for over a hundred years.

The land of Sabine, " 'tis mine," said the Americans, "by right of purchase"; " 'tis mine," said the Spanish, "by the claim of Domingo Teran Del Rio of 1690."

And so the Neutral Strip was established. Each nation begrudging the other every inch of it. A lawless land which must now be policed for the good of both nations.

The southwestern border of the United States was established by the Adams-Onis Treaty at Washington on February 22, 1821, as being the Sabine River; Adams representing the United States and Onis representing the New Republic of Mexico.

Would the settlers of the Neutral Strip and those from the Sabine River to the Rio Grande recognize the treaty of Washington? The Gutierrez-McGee filibuster expedition had proved that these people wished a new freedom. Not that of the United States or that of Mexico. Many men had cast their eyes toward the land of Texas, there was so much of it for the taking. But the Indians were not just sitting on the sideline observing what was happening, they were pressing for their rights, too, against any and all nations. Surely they realized their prize prossession was slowly slipping from them. The Indians recognized no treaty among the white men. Only the agreements with the whites which concerned their welfare was of importance to them.

Many young adventurers of all nationalities and from all walks of life had come into the area and found the excitement to their liking. They would align themselves with the side which offered them the most advantageous opportunities.

General Edmund P. Gaines found himself in a predicament when he received orders on Dec. 21, 1819, to establish a new command post near the border of the Sabine River. He was ordered "to establish a new post in a location that will protect our southwestern border as well as all of the inhabitants within the boundaries of the United States in your area."

In the Southwest area he had federal troops under his command; at New Orleans, 96 men under Major Many; at Baton Rouge, 212 officers and men; at Fort Claiborne, Natchitoches, 56 men under the command of Major Coombs; and, at Camp Sabine, on the Sabine River, 105 men under the command of General Wilkinson.

On November 15, 1820, Lieutenant Colonel Zachary Taylor and four Companies of the 7th United States Infantry had established Fort Selden on the south bank of Bayou Pierre on the highest hill in the area, one and one-half miles from the confluence of Bayou Pierre with Red River, six miles north of Natchitoches and three miles west of Grand Ecore. Taylor named the Fort, "Selden," in honor of Lieutenant Colonel Joseph Selden, who fought in the American revolution and who was at that time stationed in the Arkansas Territory.

From the vantage point of Fort Selden on Bayou Pierre there was a one-mile view of the channel of the bayou. There was flat-boat traffic on the bayou to the town of Bayou Pierre and on northward to the Petit Caddos in the vicinity of the present day city of Shreveport. Taylor was in position to control the water traffic on the bayou.*

At Fort Selden Lieutenant Colonel Taylor received this message:

Special Order No. 19.

Headquarters West Dept,
Fort Selden, Red River,
March 28, 1822.

Lieutenant Colonel Taylor with the troops under his command, will as soon as possible, occupy the position at Shields Springs, 25 miles south southwest of this place, where he will canton the troops in huts of a temporary kind. The buildings will be constructed by the troops. Supplies necessary, will be sent by the Quartermaster.

Lieutenant Colonel Taylor is charged with the south

---

*Red River at this time was blocked by log jams as far as Fort Towsin in Arkansas. Bayou Pierre was the water route as far as the vicinity of Shreveport.

western frontier of Louisiana. To defend and protect its inhabitants, as well as those of the frontier.

> Signed: Edmund P. Gaines
> Commanding General of The
> Southwest Frontier.

Order No. 20

> Headquarters, West Dept.
> Fort Selden, Red River,
> March 29, 1822.

The General congratulates the Troops on the prospects of their immediate occupation of an eligible position near the National Boundary.

> Signed: Edmund P. Gaines,
> Commanding General,
> Southwest Frontier.

These two orders confirmed a previous order issued to Taylor by Gaines in November of 1821 while he was in Arkansas— an order to explore the vicinity of Natchitoches and the Neutral Land and to locate a site for a cantonment of a permanent nature, which would be nearer the Louisiana and Texas boundary.

Lieutenant Colonel Taylor selected the site and then wrote to General Gaines informing him of his selection—on a hill which

---

OPPOSITE PAGE — Explanation of the Map of Fort Jesup. 1831.

In 1831 Fort Jesup had reached maximum in size and no new buildings were added after this date. The scale of the map thus shown, is 132 feet per inch.

A.	Dragoon Stables.	Q.	Soldier's Quarters 6 Buildings.
B.	Stable.	R.	Cottage.
C.	Blissville.	S.	Officer's Quarters—7th Inf.
D.	Soldier's Quarters—3rd Inf.	T.	Officer's Quarters.
E.	Officers Quarters—3rd Inf.	U.	Adjutant's Office.
F.	Mess House—3rd Inf.	V.	Hospital.
G.	Officers Quarters No. 1.	W.	Kitchens to Soldier's Quarters.
H.	Officers Quarters No. 2.	Y.	Soldier's Quarters.
I.	Officers Quarters No. 3.	X.	Band's Quarters.
J.	Store House.	Z.	Officer's Quarters.
K.	Powder Magazine.	P.	Parade Grounds.
L.	Guard House.	- - - - - - -	El Camino Real.
M.	Adjutant's Office—3rd Inf.		Note: Today's Museum is a replica
N.	Quarter Master's Office.		of one of the buildings listed as Z and
O.	Quarter Master's Office.		Kitchen is original of those listed as
P.	Commissionary Store.		W.

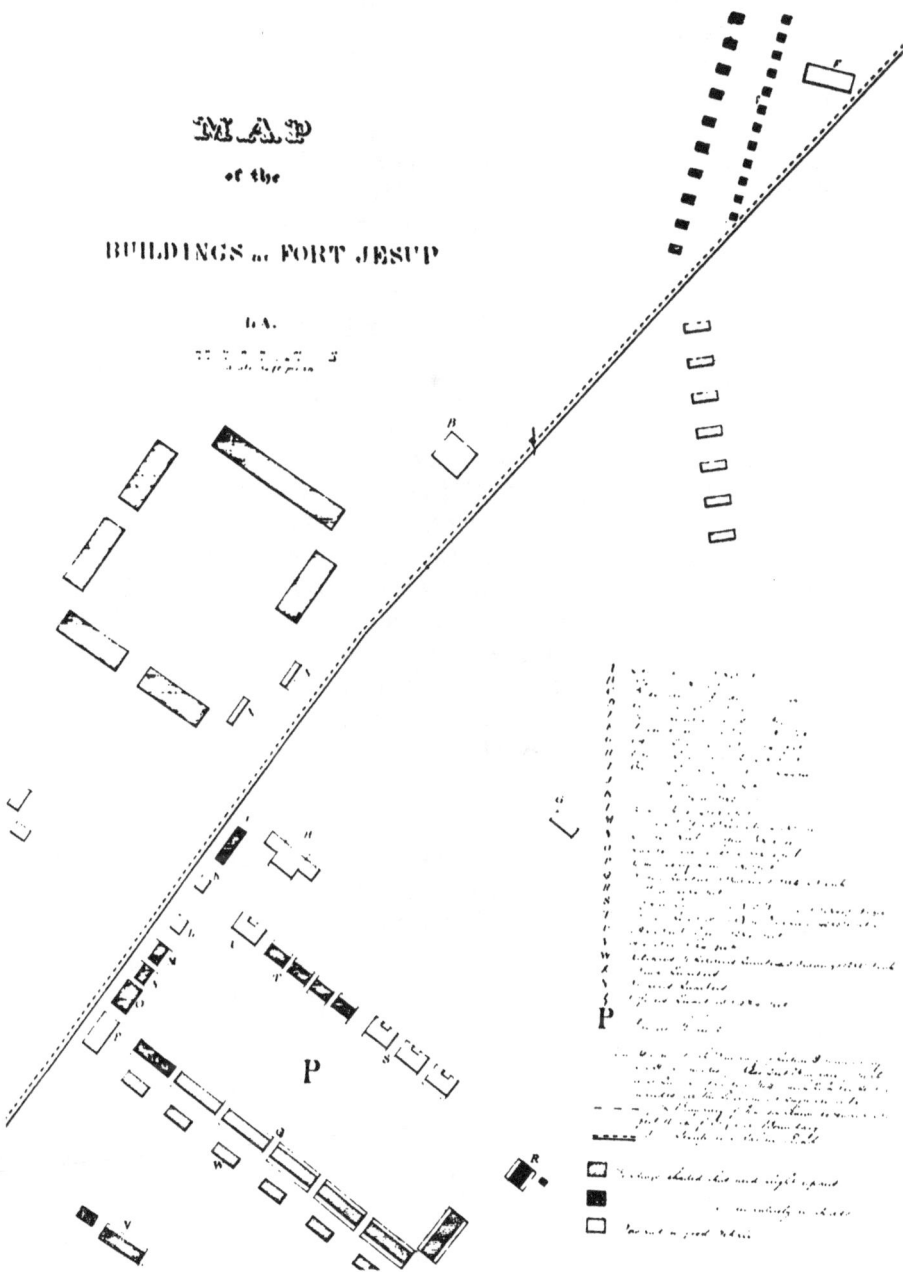

MAP

of the

BUILDINGS at FORT JESUP

LA.

P

P

P

was the division between the watersheds of the Red River and the Sabine River. He went as far as he could to the west to establish a permanent command post. Camp Sabine on Sabine River which was established by General Wilkinson was not considered a permanent position, but only an encampment for the benefit of the United States Police Patrol established in the Neutral Strip to police the Sabine River border and to look after the safety of the settlers within the area known as The Neutral Land.

General Wilkinson and his detachment were never entirely successful in quelling the activities of the lawless element. Federal troops stationed at Sabine Town or Camp Sabine or Sabine Block-house (all one and the same site) had some 5000 square miles of territory to patrol. A patrol at that time would have consisted of ten mounted men and one officer. There were approximately 112 men and officers at Camp Sabine, and the detachment post would have consisted of ten patrols. If all were in activity at the same time each patrol would have had 500 square miles to patrol, which, of course, was an impossible task. At this time there were about 50 men and officers in Natchitoches at Fort Claiborne and even the two combined groups would not have been adequate for policing such an enormous area. The outlaws knew this and in the Neutral Strip the lawless roamed and pillaged at will and remained hidden in its thousands of hills and hollows.

It is interesting to note that at the time of the battle of New Orleans in 1815 General Jackson thought the Neutral Strip frontier so important that he did not withdraw the troops from that post to assist in the battle with the British.

In 1822 when Lieuenant Colonel Zachary Taylor established a cantonment at Jesup at Shields Spring by the order of General Edmund Pendleton Gaines, on the highest hill between the Sabine River and the Red River, he had taken into consideration the claim of Cavalier Robert de La Salle, when in 1682, this Frenchman claimed all the land drained by that river for the King of France. With the Louisiana purchase, which consisted of all land claimed by France west of the Mississippi River, this would include the site of Cantonment Jesup on that hilltop. The rainwater falling on the western slope would drain into the Mississippi River via Bayou Adais and Bonna Vista into Bayou Dupont to Little River to Bayou Pierre to the Red River and thence into the Mississippi River. Waters falling on the western slope would find the way to the Sabine River via Phillips Bayou to Bayou LaNann, thence to the Sabine River. Thus, the establishment of Cantonment Jesup at this particular spot had argumentative value in favor of the United States against any outcome of the melting-pot development which could arise west of the Sabine River.

By November 9, 1822, the Quartermaster General's report stated that the Federal militia was consolidated and located at the Garrison Post at Baton Rouge, three hundred fifteen officers and men of the First Infantry; and at Cantonment Jesup, one hundred forty-one officers and men of four companies of the seventh Infantry under the command of Lieutenant Colonel Zachary Taylor.

1822 marked the end of the detachment at Sabine Town, Fort Selden on Bayou Pierre, near Grand Ecore, Louisiana and Fort Claiborne at Natchitoches, Louisiana.

When Mexico won her independence in 1821 the Empressario System was continued and by the end of the year 1823, Stephen Fuller Austin had executed the grant which had previously been given to his father, Moses Austin, in which nearly three hundred American families were allowed to settle in the Texas area. Colonel James B. Many, Commandante at Cantonment Jesup, was there to greet the emigrants on their way to Texas. The same year General Gaines decreed that Cantonment Jesup would be known as Fort Jesup, and made it a permanent establishment of the Army of the United States Government, which resulted in a more thorough settlement of the Sabine area known as the Neutral Strip.

Shawneetown, two miles to the west of Fort Jesup on El Camino Real, came into existence to supply the evil demands of the immediate area—gambling, horse-racing and other auxillaries of dis-order.

The twenty-five-mile house, or Midway House, two miles east of Fort Jesup on the road to Natchitoches was a wayside tavern and Inn.

By 1826 the Mexican Republic had forbidden further immigration into Texas—the direct result of a contract which had been acquired by Hayden Edwards to establish eight hundred families in the Nacogdoches area. Here Edwards organized the short-lived Republic of Freedonia which resulted from the Freedonia Rebellion. Edwards was driven out of the Nacogdoches area and his contract revoked.

In this same year a letter, originating at Fort Jesup, to the Governor of Louisiana, appeared in the Natchitoches Courier, one of the two newspapers published at Natchitoches at that time, answering the President of the United States, who wanted to know about the possibility of establishing steam navigation on the Red River above the Town of Natchitoches. A duplicate of the original, which sent to the President, was placed at the disposal of the Natchitoches Courier. Colonel James B. Many at Fort Jesup wished the local citizens of the area to know that the personnel at Fort Jesup was useful in ways other than military.

> The Natchitoches Courier
> Fort Jesup
> Natchitoches, Louisiana
> March 13, 1826

Captain Berch and Lieutenant Lee with a detachment of men from Fort Jesup, have been up the Red River examining the great rafts of debris which block the channel of Red River. This detachment returned a few days ago after an absence on that duty of about two months. We have conversed with these scientific and learned gentlemen on the subject of their excursion, the object of which was to ascertain the practicability of opening steamboat traffic through or around these obstructions.

They report that in a distance of one hundred miles above the Town of Natchitoches, there are 181 log jams, ranging from ten yards in length to a distance of one-half mile. To clear these obstructions would be a tremendous and expensive task.

I wish to be remindful that in as much as the Sabine River which lies west of this place, usually maintains enough water to afford its usage by steamboats. In these trying times such as exists between ourselves and our neighbors to the west, I think it advisable that such an excursion be made up the Sabine River, for military if not to mention commercial purposes.

Signed: Colonel James B. Many,
Commander of the Southwest
Teritory, Fort Jesup,
Natchitoches, Louisiana.*

In the same newspaper on this date appeared the advertisement: "Just arrived on the Steamship-Packet, *Superior*, Captain Alex Le Sardo, Master."

And in the same paper on the same date was an advertisement of John Baldwin's Store on El Camino Real:

"Liquors—Maderia, Teneriff, Malaga, Claret wines, Cognac, Brandy, Holland and English Gins, West Indian Rum, Old and Common whiskey, coffee and tea. Loaf lump and brown sugar. 100 sacks of salt. Boots, Shoes and Headwear. Cravats, Shawls, Collars and Cuffs (In Sets), Handkerchiefs and Lace. Belts, Ribbons and Buckles. Full and half cotton and wool hose. Mosquito bars. English gingham. Satins—black and blue. Bleached and unbleached cotton shirting. Modes de Fasion Casimers, Fancy Calicoes, Superior, friction-matches. Arm and Leg Garters.

Medicines 1/2 bbl. of hops, Jujube and Pectoral pastes, Swain's Panacea, Stillman's Sasparilla pills, Liverwort, Arrowroot, Horehound, Southern Cough drops, New England Cough Syrup, Oldridge's Balm-Columbia, Lavender Water and Rose Water.

Ready to wear trousers and overcoats from $1.00 to

---

*If the address of Natchitoches, Louisiana, appearing as the address of Fort Jesup seems strange, it must be remembered that at that time Natchitoches was the nearest Post-office.

$25.00. Tobacco for chewing and smoking. Extra sweet Havana cigars.

Exquisite Organdies and Embroideries.

Harness Buckles and Pistols. Also Suspenders and Corsets, $1.00 each.

John Baldwin with his wife and two daughters must have established their store prior to 1826. The location of the Baldwin Store marked the site of the later town of Many, Louisiana, which derives its name from Colonel James B. Many. Baldwin's Store, Tavern, Inn and Blacksmith Shop comprised the area of the Stille home and the present sites of the Sabine State Bank & Trust Co., and The Peoples State Bank in Many.

During this period Manuel and Jose Chellettre operated the "Two Brothers' Freight Line" between Natchitoches and Nacogdoches. Also at this time the firm of Barr and Davenport had a freight line service between the same two destinations.

The newspaper also listed the names of the steamboats which were vying for the Natchitoches-Texas trade: *The Florence, The Superior, The Alexander, The Chesapeak, The Courtland, The Eliza, The Governor Shelby, The Hornet, The Kiamechi, The Plaquemine, The Raven, The Teche, The Telegraph, The Shepardess* and *The Arkansas*.

Henry Stoker, having received a government land grant, had by now established his home, and he enlarged his holdings by trading eleven horses for land belonging to several families of the Adais Indians who were living near his homestead.

Fort Jesup during its existence trained such men as Second Lieutenant Phil Sheridan, Lieutenant Thomas Lawson, Captain Bragg, Lt. L. B. E. Bonneville, Lt. James E. Goins, Captain Davie E. Twiggs, Capt. J. Hardee, and Lt. Rufus Ingalls. These men during the war between the states, became generals either for the North or the South. Lieutenant U. S. Grant, who was stationed at Camp Salubrity near Grand Ecore, was often a visitor at Fort Jesup.

Such important men as David Crockett, James Bowie, Stephen F. Austin and Sam Houston; and such famous scouts

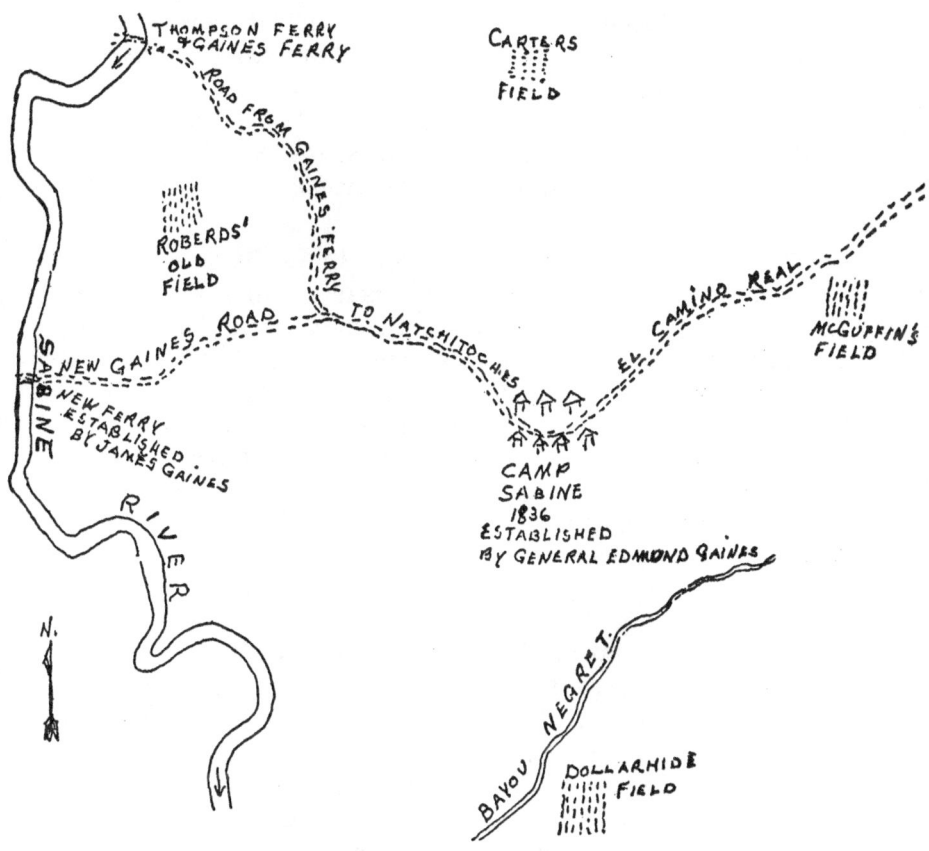

Map of Area Around
Camp Sabine — 1836

as Ben S. Lilly and "Big Foot" Wallace visited there. Because they were welcomed and entertained at Fort Jesup, accusations were made by the Spanish that Fort Jesup was a meeting place for those planning the overthrow of the Mexican government. And this may very well have been true, for supplies necessary for the conduct of the war for Texas independence undoubtedly passed through Fort Jesup.

There is evidence that the United States did render secret support to the fighting Texans in their struggle for independence. This fort at such a strategic location could have blocked revolutionary movements in this frontier area if it had chosen to do so. Because of this Fort Jesup became recognized as the heart of the Texas-Mexican revolution. The garrison at Fort Jesup assisted by checking the border Indians of Louisiana, Arkansas and northern Texas, who may have otherwise aided the Mexican forces against the retreating Sam Houston just before the Battle of San Jacinto.

THE GAINES MILITARY ROAD, 1827-1828

The Military Road or The Gaines Military Road, sometimes referred to as General Jackson's road, connected the two most remote western outposts of the United States' army, Fort Jesup and Fort Towsin. This last was located at the confluence of the Kiamechi River of Oklahoma and the Red River. The military road was nearly three hundred miles long.

In 1831 Fort Jesup came under the command of Brevet Brigadier General Leavenworth, with six companies of the Seventh Infantry. In 1832 the garrison was increased to two hundred ninety-six men and officers, and Colonel James B. Many again assumed command.

It was during the command of Gen. Leavenworth that some of the settlers or squatters that had moved into the area, some within a half-mile distance of the Fort, made themselves objectionable by selling whiskey to the personnel at Fort Jesup. In order that the sale of whiskey near the fort might be stopped the following order was issued:

Order No. 69

To all whom it may concern:

Having received instructions from General Leavenworth to take possession for the United States, for the purpose of supplying fuel for the garrison, of all public land within three miles of the flagstaff of Fort Jesup; all persons having a "donation or pre-emption" claim are hereby ordered to vacate the said premises immediately, or at the earliest possible date, otherwise they will be dealt with according to the law.

Signed: Francis Lee
Acting Assistant Quartermaster
U. S. Army

Fort Jesup, Louisiana, 7th November, 1831.

XVI

TEXAS AND INDEPENDENCE
1831 - 1836

James Bowie, David Crockett and Sam Houston were entertained at Fort Jesup by Colonel Many while en-route to cast their lot with the Texans. To greet these men in Nacogdoches were Thomas J. Rusk, Frost Thorn, Adolphus Sterne, Charles S. Taylor, Henry Raguet, Doctor Irion, John Drust and William C. Logan, all of whom were to have a hand in winning the Texas independence.

The municipality of San Augustine was organized in 1833, and was the first town in Texas to be laid out on the American plan of forty-eight blocks, consisting of three hundred fifty-six feet with streets forty feet wide, and two lots in the center for the Courthouse.

The history of San Augustine dates back to the very earliest Texas history, with its location astradle the El Camino Real, previously the Buffalo Trail and then part of the Caddo Indian trail system. Cabeza de Vaca passed this spot and later a scouting party of the Hernando de Soto expedition. The Ais (Ayist) Indians were there to greet the Domingo Teran Del Rios Expedition and then the Domingo Ramone Expedition. The Ais Indians of San Augustine were the first Texas Indians to establish trade agreements with the French, when in 1708 the Frenchman, Bejoux, began trading with them for horses.

San Augustine became a most important port of entry, second only to Galveston. It may very well be called the Cradle of Texas Independence for it is said that any man entering San

Fort St. Jean Baptiste Des Natchitoches.

This interpretation of how Fort St. Jean Baptiste looked was drawn by the architects, Butler and Dobson of Natchitoches, for the Committee for the Restoration of Colonial Natchitoches, Inc.

It is my sincere hope that this restoration will be executed by the year 1964 when Natchitoches will in that year celebrate her 250th anniversary.

To the Frenchmen of that period, the title, Fort St. Jean Baptiste des Natchitoches, meant that the Fort or Post was named for St. John The Baptist and that its location was among the Natchitoches Indians.

It was this Fort which St. Denis defended against the Natchez Indians in 1731.

Old Kitchen at Fort Jesup—only remaining building of the original fort.

Augustine, be he French, Spanish or American, became a Texan. Ninety percent of the men who engaged in the strife for Texas independence had walked the streets of San Augustine.

The progress of the struggle for Texas independence was watched with keenest interest throughout the United States, but the interest south of the Mason-Dixon line was greater as most of the Texas settlers came from the Southern states.

Louis Cass, the Secretary of War, on January 23, 1835, sent instructions to Major General Edmund P. Gaines, ordering him to move to a position nearer the western frontier of Louisiana, and to assume personal command of the troops near the Mexican (Texas) border. Blockhouses were erected to protect the supplies of the personnel of the camp. General Gaines took personal command of the troops there.

The Red River by the year 1835 had changed its course and taken the Bayou Rigolet de Bon Dieux as its main channel, leaving Natchitoches high and dry except during the spring and winter months. The river port of Grand Ecore then became the most important shipping port for the southwestern area of Louisiana and eastern Texas. The Texas trail now by-passed Natchitoches some four miles to the west, connecting it with Grand Ecore.

General Gaines wrote of the decaying condition of the buildings at Fort Jesup, and acquired a twenty-five thousand dollar appropriation for their repair through the help of Thomas S. Jesup, Quartermaster General of the United States, who had been given the honor of having Fort Jesup named after him.

General Gaines possessed a war-like nature and he nourished the idea of annexing Texas in one blaze of glory for himself. Further, he knew that President Andrew Jackson wanted Texas as a part of the United States.

Gaines, in a letter to Cass, stated that B. F. Palmer and William Palmer, living near Fort Jesup, had informed him that a Spaniard had arrived at the house of one of their neighbors, saying he had been commissioned by Santa Anna to go among the Caddos and other upper Red River tribes of Indians and stir them up into attacking the upper settlements of Texas.

Gaines had sent Lieutenant Bonnel with Eusebia Cartinez, to gain the good will of the Caddos without success. But they were successful among the Indians further to the west of the Caddos. They learned that Manuel Flores, who had established at Spanish-Town between Fort Jesup and Natchitoches, won alliances with the Caddos.

Enclosed in the letter were communications from Henry Raguet, Chairman of the Committee of Vigilance at Nacogdoches and A. Hotchkiss, Chairman of a similar committee at San Augustine, both declaring that Indians had moved into the area along El Camino Real and requesting an investigation.

Cass was informed that the Alamo had fallen and many of the troops, including Fannin, were killed near Goliad on the Madina River and that Sam Houston was in full retreat toward the Louisiana border.

Gaines now received orders to use his own judgment about the affairs on the frontier, and that if he had to go into the Texas territory to insure the peace of the frontier, he could go no further than Nacogdoches.

Gaines was still at Sabine Blockhouse when word came that on April 18, 1836, Sam Houston had defeated Santa Anna at San Jacinto Bay. Thus Gaines' chance for glory was gone. However, he must be credited with a timely move, when a few weeks before he had ordered troops to Nacogdoches, thus spoiling the counterpunch attempted by Santa Anna to stir up the Indians. This, without a doubt, quelled the prospective uprising of the Indians.

TREATY WITH THE CADDO INDIANS

In June, 1835, Colonel Many sent a contingent of soldiers to the upper Red River country to lend assistance in the signing and execution of the treaty between the United States and the Caddo Indians. At the Caddo Indian Agency house, located on a bluff overlooking Bayou Pierre, nine miles south of the present-day city of Shreveport, was drawn an agreement with the Indians, dated July 1, 1835:

The Chiefs, Headmen and Warriors of the tribes of the Caddo Nation of Indians, agree to cede and relinquish to the United States all land contained in the following boundaries: Bounded on the west by the North-south line which separates Louisiana and the United States from the Republic of Mexico and on the west by the Red River in the Territory of Louisiana and Arkansas.

The Chiefs, Headmen and Warriors agree to relinquish their possession of the land and agree to move out of the boundaries of the United States at their own expense, and never to return to live, settle, or establish themselves as a nation or a community.

In consideration the Caddo Nation will be paid $30,000 in goods and horses as agreed upon and $10,000 to be paid per annum in money, each year, for the four years following. Making a whole sum of $80,000, paid and payable.

In Testimony Whereof, the said Jehiel Brooks, Commissioner, the Chiefs, Headmen and Warriors of the Caddo Nation, have hereunto set their hands and affixed their seals.

Signed: Jehiel Brooks

Tarshar	His X Mark	Tehowahinno	His X Mark
Tasauninot	His X Mark	Tooeksoach	His X Mark
Saliownhown	His X Mark	Tehowainia	His X Mark
Tennehinun	His X Mark	Sauninow	His X Mark
Oat	His X Mark	Saunivaot	His X Mark
Tinnowin	His X Mark	Highahidock	His X Mark
Chowabah	His X Mark	Mattan	His X Mark
Kianhoon	His X Mark	Towabimneh	His X Mark
Tialesun	His X Mark	Aach	His X Mark
Tehowawinow	His X Mark	Sookiantow	His X Mark
Tewinnun	His X Mark	Sohone	His X Mark
Kardy	His X Mark	Ossinse	His X Mark
Tiohtow	His X Mark		

In the Presence of:

Thomas J. Harrison, Capt, 3rd Regt Inf.
Commander of Detachment from Fort Jesup, Louisiana.

J. Bonnell, 1st Lieut, 3rd Regt Inf.,
Fort Jesup, Louisiana.

G. P. Frile, 2nd Lieut, 3rd Regt Inf.,
Fort Jesup, Louisiana.

D. M. Heard, M. D., Acting Assistant Surgeon,
U. S. A., Fort Jesup, Louisiana.

Isaac C. Williamson, Citizen.
Henry Queen, Citizen.
John P. Edwards, Interpreter.

Other Recommendations:

Articles supplementary to Treaty, whereas: The said Indian Nation gave to Francois Grappe and his three (3) sons, then born and still living named, Jacques, Dominique and Balthazar, in the year 1801, one league of land to each, according to the Spanish custom. This being a total of four square leagues of land.

Larken Edwards, being old and unable to work and having been a steadfast friend of the Caddo Indians, was also given at the request of the Indians, land which now comprises most of the area of present day Shreveport, Louisiana.

On May 14, 1837, the following ad appeared in the Red River Gazette, a Natchitoches newspaper:

A. W. P. Ussery has the pleasure to inform friends and the public that he has taken the Fort Jesup Hotel and is now ready for company. He has a commodious house and stable and a delightful-situation. In addition to the comforts of the well regulated house, the weary traveler will be regaled at night and morning by the delightful music of the Fort Jesup Band.

With the ability of Texas to maintain her independence, Fort Jesup settled down to the humdrum existence of a peaceful, frontier post. In the summer of 1838 the garrison was reduced to two companies of men and officers. In 1840 the third infantry members at Fort Jesup were ordered to Florida. This left one company of fourth infantry at Fort Jesup.

Texas threw open its doors to immigrants and daily these pased through the Fort Jesup area, to travel El Camino Real westward. Many, however, stopped in the Natchitoches-Sabine country. Texans knew that immigrants represented power, power to resist Mexico.

This peaceful existence was not to last long. There was talk of the annexation of Texas by the United States which Mexico did not want. For as long as Texas was a Republic there was a possibility that Mexico might recover this prize possession, a possession which also included the present states of New Mexico and a part of Wyoming.

As early as 1843 the United States was contemplating acquiring Texas as a state. In the meantime they had purchased the territory of New Mexico, Utah, Nevada and Wyoming from Texas which did not set well with the Republic of Mexico. There was a kind of cold friendship existing between the United States and Mexico.

Late in 1843 General Zachary Taylor was ordered to the Texas-Louisiana frontier, thus early in 1844 there came to Fort Jesup the Army of Observation.

Camp Salubrity was established three miles west of Grand Ecore on the Texas Road May 18, 1844, where the fourth infantry companies were encamped. One of the young officers was Lieutenant U. S. Grant.

On May 18, 1845, General Taylor at Fort Jesup received a letter marked "Confidential" from Secretary of War, Marcey. This secretly and officially marked the beginning of the disposition of troops and the laying of plans for the war with Mexico. Marcey wrote, "I am directed by the President to cause forces now under your command and those which may be assigned, to be put into position where they may most promptly act in the defense of Texas."

At Fort Jesup under the command of General Taylor were seven companies of the Second Dragoons and eight companies of the Fourth Infantry. Four companies of the Fourth Infantry were stationed at Camp Salubrity.

Texas expressed a desire at the July 1845 session of the Texas Congress to become a State of the Union.

General Taylor at Fort Jesup received instructions to place the Troops under his command in the Army of Observation in such locations that would be most advantageous to render support to Texas if such an occasion should arise.

The Mexican conflict seemed inevitable and Taylor ordered Camp Salubrity abandoned and the Companies of Infantry there boarded steamboats at Grand Ecore for New Orleans along with three companies of the four companies of the 4th infantry which were stationed at Fort Jesup.

This July 1845 Report from Fort Jesup explains the removal of the Troops from Fort Jesup and those who remained:

July 17, 1845, The 3rd Infantry under the command of Lt. Col. Hitchcock left this post for the point of embarkation for New Orleans.

July 25, 1945, The 2nd Dragoons under the command of Colonel Twiggs left this post for Texas Via the Texas Trail. On this day Lt. Zill P. Inge assumes command at Fort Jesup.

There remains at this Post, and all present accounted for the following: One Company of the 4th infantry and one company of the 2nd Dragoons. The names of these men appear on the July 31, 1845, Daily Report.

Conally Triche.	Reubin W Brenner.	Isaac Trotter.
George S Darto.	William Hearne.	William McGill.
Quims Tomas.	John B Rezzer.	Berman Wellenbrook.
James Huntly.	Alexinder Silves.	William Taylor.
William Story.	James Sheene.	Edward Melton.
James Welsh.	Charles W Williams.	Gregory Bishop.
Francis Shaw.	John Adams.	John Goodele.
Samuel Tacker.	William Bayer.	Robinson McClellan.
George Waggoner.	James Heath.	Michale Ryan.
Andrew Munscle.	Michael O'Keefe.	Archibald Turner.
John A Goddard.	William R Smith.	Samuel Turner.
Benjiman Peterson.	John Mitchele.	John Freeman.
David S Barslette.	John W. Conway.	George Hendricks.
John McDormott.	William Stansbury.	Hamilton Taylor.
Joseph McGee.	Jeremiach O'Leary.	James Doughtry.
Richard Goldring.	William Bailey.	Asa Freleigh.
Samuel H. Jordan.	James Long.	William Pully.
James Conway.	Edward Harrington.	Francis Gillam.
Ferdinand Turkels.	Patrick Connally.	William R Keeper
Thurman Patterson.	Thomas Kelley.	Henry Burrows.
Michael Sheridan.	Peter Savage.	Joseph R Steward.
William H McDonnald.	William Ashton.	John Dorian.
Isaac Curry.	Stephen Turner.	Frederick Leach.
John L Creps.	Joseph A Jinkins.	William Turner.
John B Hickey.	Patrick Maloney.	Alexander Cody.
John Murphy.	George Holmes.	William A Burks.
Paul Spencer.	Louis H Tucker.	John Hunter.
Hugh McHugh.	John Hamilton.	Phillip Hoffman.
John R Bloomer.	James Horton.	Richard A Banks
William Horton.	James Foley.	Patrick Bigland
Cazimiery Rosinowski.	Horice Clark.	Charles W Livingston.
George Cassody.	William Howe.	
Ames W Grimes		

These men comprise the 1st Company of the 2nd Dragoons and One half Company of the 3rd Inf. and one half Company of the 4th infantry. Most of them were sick at the time of the dispersement of the troops at Fort Jesup.

Signed:

1st Lt Zill P Inge
1st Co 2nd Dragoons.
Fort Jesup, La.

July 31 1845.

On November 29, 1845, the Adjutant General ordered that Fort Jesup was no longer required as a military post, all military supplies, buildings and land be disposed of.

Thus Zachary Taylor when a Lt. Col. executed the order to establish Fort Jesup and 23 years later as a Brigadier General executed the order to abandon it.

Ironic as it may seem, Fort Jesup brought law to a lawless land. It was a buffer zone through which passed softly, those intent on a new kind of freedom. It was the mould which shaped the southwestern section of these United States.

old Ambroise Sompayrac House. Natchitoches chief depot for trade with Mexico, early 1800's Washington St. at Pavie on River .. demolished in 1900.

If one must in a few words offer a summation of all that has passed before . . . . . Then.

This tiny spot, in Louisiana's vast domain,
High on a hill-top, a memory to remain.
Redbuds and Dogwood, bring spring's tender smile,
To a land so fertile, it rivals that of the Nile.
Yonder, the Red's mighty currents roll.
Gleaming, sparkling, rivaling Hidalgo's Gold.

In a grove, where the stately Pine trees tower,
Blending with the Oak, the Ash and wild Flower,
Quickly, their lips meet and arms entwine,
Secluded they are, by the Rattan-vine,
This love doesn't any boundary know.
The Savage speaks, 'tis time to go.

They match wits, the Hidalgo and the Fleur de Lys.
Fiesta and Fandangero, invited, they all come to see.
This Wilderness Road, which both Friend and Enemy Travel
This intricate-mess, shall two men unravel
From Crescent-City to Natchitoches and on to Mexico,
Past Los Adais and Presidios, must Saint and Sinner go.

This Land—'tis Mine, 'tis Yours, 'tis Mine.
To the Stars and Stripes the Savage states, 'twas Mine.
To his God, Ayandt Daddi, in a blanketed-blue sky,
He looks and he questions, "Whither goest I?"
To his people, his eyes reflect his fears,
Caddo generosity paid, with "A Trail of Tears."

ADDENDA

LAND GRANTS

In 1816 the United States Land Office sent representatives to Natchitoches, although previously representatives had been in Natchitoches in 1806 to register land claims within the Neutral Strip area. Proof was demanded of people settling land in the Neutral Strip, referring to either French or Spanish grants.

In 1730 Zavallez, then Governor of Los Adais, granted three square leagues of land to Manuel Sanchez on Los Pedro Creek (Bayou Pierre), the grant was listed as La Nana de Los Rio Pedro. (Note: The wife of St. Denis was a Sanchez, her mother being Maria Esperrillo Sanchez before her marriage to Don Diago Ramone). The Sanchez Grant is also referred to as Los Tres Llanos (Three Plains) was approved again in 1742 by Governor Larros in the name of Governor Winthusin. The son of Manuel Sanchez was eighty two years of age when in 1832 a clear title was issued by the United States Land Office. The Sanchez family had lived on the land 102 years before they obtained a clear title to it.

Juan De Mora was granted one league square of land on Bayou Dupont at Los Adais by Zavallez which is the land located in an area known today as "Fish Pond Bottom."

Testimony of Gregoria Mora before the land office officials shows: "This is a receipt of tithes I collected on land west of the Calcasieu River, West of Bayou Kisachey and west of Arroyo Hondo. Also west of Bayou Pedro (Bayou Pierre) dated in Nacogdoches, Feb. 27, 1797, and signed by Jose Maria Guadiana (Rubric)

Owner of Land	Location
Pablo Lifita	Los Pedros Creek (Bayou Pierre)
Andres Balentine	" " " " "
Jose Lavina	Los Cebellas Prairie
Pedro Dolet	Los Adais Creek (Winn Creek)
Antonio Dubois	" " " " "
Francisco Prudhomme	In village of Adais Indians, one mile north of Robeline near site of the Presidio de Los Adais.
Francisco Morban (Der Bonne)	Dorango Creek (west of the village of Allen and three miles northwest of the village of Shamrock)
Widdow of Tontin Bisson	On Topolcot Creek at Allen site, near Leroy Anderson Plantation
Manuel Prudhomme	On Lago Ocosa Near Cypress, Louisiana
Marfil	On Lago de Los Adais (Spanish Lake)
Francois Rouquier	West of Lago Tierre Noir (Sibley Lake)
Santiago Wallace (Englishman)	On San Juan Creek (Bay St. John in the Lake Charles area)
Jose Piernas	At Santo Maria Adelaide (vicinity of Zwolle, Louisiana)

CLAIM OF PEDRO DOLET, FRENCHMAN (Pierre Dole)

On December 29, 1795, I, Jose Cayetano de Zepede, executor to Los Adais and by request of Antonio Gil y Barbo Governor of Texas at Nacogdoches, went with my assistant, Don Jose de La Vega to a place at Los Adais, where a petitioner had built a home there. I granted this land.

> He pulled up Grass,
> Planted Stakes,
> Threw dust into the air,

To show his possession.

I have granted this land and designate the aforesaid tract of land as "San Pedro de Los Adais."

Signed:
Don Luis de La Vega.   Jose Cayeleno de Zepeda
Vincente Del Rio   Executor

CLAIM OF EDWARD MURPHY

Don Edwardo Murphy, petitioner from the post at Natchitoches, states that on a creek La Petit St. Jean and Reo Hondo I find advantageous to collect my cattle, I humbly ask of you to give me possession of this land.

Nacogdoches, October 17, 1791. In consequence of petitioner and that the land solicited is in the province of Texas and vacant I do grant in due best form and that it may so appear.

Signed:
Antonio Gil y Barbo

(Note: This tract of land was in the area of southwest from the Country Club of Natchitoches on Highway 1 North).

CLAIM OF EDWARD MURPHY FOR THE FIRM OF MURPHY, SMITH, BARR AND DAVENPORT

Edward Murphy, Leander Smith, William Barr, Samuel Davenport. (District Judge William Murray heard the plea of the Firm of Murphy, Smith, Davenport and Barr).

August 1, 1798, Don Jose Guadiana, Governor at Nacogdoches, granted to Don Edward Murphy a grant of land named "La Nana Prairie" located seven leagues east of the Rio Sabinas on the road to Natchitoches, 144 sections of land astraddle El Camino Real (a 12 square mile land grant, extending eastward from Bayou Lana and could have very well taken the townsite of Many, Louisiana. Murphy transferred this land to the above mentioned firm, November 3, 1798).

CLAIM OF MICHEL CROW

Michel Crow, son of Isaac Crow, who wed the widow Chabineau of the Post at Natchitoches, bought the land of Miguel Viciente which has been granted to Miguel Viciente in 1769 by Governor Hugo O'Connor, who was at that time Governor of

Los Adais and all of the Texas country. The grant was listed as San Miguel de Los Rio Patrice and was located on the Sabine River and Patrice Creek in the northwest portion of Sabine Parish.

One incident in which an arrest and the results of which served as evidence in favor of the victim occurred while Lieutenant Zebulon M. Pike was in command of a police patrol of the Neutral Strip in 1806, when he arrested Michel Crow and brought him to the post at Natchitoches, accusing him of contraband operations to and from the Texas country. Captain Bernardino Mantero, leading a Spanish patrol with the assistance of Lieutenants Pike and McGee, came to the ranchero of Michael Crow and upon questioning Crow's wife and her two sons, learned of the actions of Lieutenant Pike previously. Captain Mantero went to Natchitoches and declared that Crow was innocent of such charges and that the unfortunate Crow was only engaged in farming and ranching; further the Spanish did not have Crow's name on the list of traders in contrabrand known to the Spanish at Nacogdoches, thus, when Michel Crow registered his claim for land, he had proof of the length of time he had resided there taken from the arrest papers.

CLAIM OF THE HEIRS OF WIDOW TONTIN

In 1791 Anthanase De Mezieres granted to Julian and Pierre Bisson land called Ecore Rouge (Red Hill) located at the present day hamlet of Allen between Robeline and Powhattan, Louisiana, one hundred ninety square arpents of land on each side of Topelcot Bayou. The widow Tontin, nee Possiot, wed Julian Bisson (Note: The store at Allen and the home of Leroy—Dobber—Anderson are located atop Ecore Rouge).

CLAIM OF THE HEIRS OF ANTHANASE POISSOT

In 1792, Anthanase De Mezieres, Governor of the Texas region at Natchitoches Post, granted land to Anthanase Poissot in recognition of his claim of having bought the land of La Tres Cabanes (Three Cabins) from Chief Antoine of the Hyatasses (Yatassee Indians) on Bayou Pierre.

An exact reproduction of one of the officers quarters at Fort Jesup which now houses the relics pertaining to the fort.

Fort Jesup, originally "Cantonment Jesup," was established in the spring of 1821, by Lieutenant Colonel Zachary Taylor, who was executing the orders of Major General Edmund Pendleton Gaines. Taylor had under his command four companies of the United States 7th Infantry.

On November 29, 1845 the Adjutant General ordered that Fort Jessup was no longer required as a military post and that all military supplies, buildings and land be disposed of.

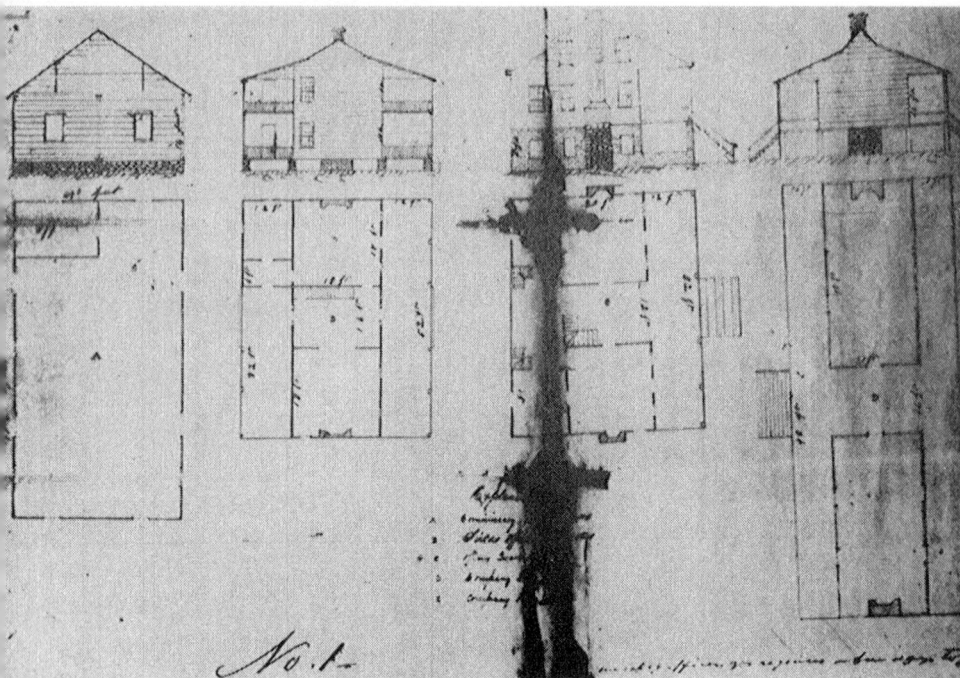

Original plans of Fort Jesup
1. Mess Hall
2. Enlisted Men's Quarters
3. Officers' Quarters

Officers' Quarters—another view.

CLAIM OF THE FIRM OF MURPHY, SMITH, DAVENPORT AND BARR

The Los Ormegas Land Grant of Jacinto Mora contained two hundred seven thousand three hundred sixty acres bordering on the east bank of the SabineRiver and astradle El Camino Real. The grant was issued by Jose Cayeleno de Zepeda, Governor at Nacogdoches and was sold to the above mentioned firm in 1805. The land was transferred under the title of Santa Marie Adeliade Ormegas, but was not recognized by the United States Government until 1842.

CLAIM OF THE HEIRS OF
PIERRE GAINNIE (PEDRO GANE) (PIER GAGNIER)
HIPOLITE BORDELON
FRANCOIS GRAPPE (FRANCISCO GREBB) (FRANQUIS GREBBE)

These three men bought the land of the Chescher Indians (The area comprises the Mibermel Ranch near Powhattan, Louisiana, and the area of Three League Bayou or Nine Mile Bayou).

This grant was recognized by Anthanase DeMezieres of the Post at Natchitoches.

FAMILIES OF THE NEUTRAL STRIP (1805)

Records of Diago Maria Morfil, representing the Spanish of that area, in lieu of Jacinto Mora, directive of the Governor at Nacogdoches of the Texas Region, presented this record of families considered under the jurisdiction of Presidio Neustra Senora Del Pilar de Los Adais to the United States Land Agents in 1816:

Don Marcelo de Soto, farmer, wife, Dona Maries Baillio, Frenchwoman, two sons, two daughters, resided on Los Pedro Creek (Bayou Pierre).

Pedro Lafita, Spanish, wife, Louise Gainnie, Frenchwoman, resided on Bayou Los Tres Leagues.

Luis Beltran, Frenchman, resided on Rio Hondo. (Young's Bayou) or Bayou La Jeune. (Unmarried)

Vincente Rolan, Frenchman, wed Melanie Vascoque, Frenchwoman, residing on Bayou Durange. (This bayou drains

Cypress Swamp and empties into Topelcot Creek, also known as Cypress Swamp, Hall Break area, n o r t h of Marthaville, Louisiana).

Don Antainse Possiot, Frenchman, wed to Juanna Elena Pabi, Frenchwoman. Note: This is the Anthanase Poissot who bought land from the Chescher Indians on Three League Bayou, which extended westward to Bayou Pierre.

Michael Rambin, Frenchman wed to Theresa Baillio (Theresa Baillio, sister to Maria Baillio who wed Marcelo De Soto) resided on Los Pedros Creek (Bayou Pierre). There was one hired hand on this farm, Jose Crafon, Spanish.

Jean Balbado, Frenchman wed to Lenore Tessier, Frenchwoman, resided on Arroyo Hondo (Hagewood or Coldwater vicinity between Robeline and Natchitoches, Louisiana).

Jean Tessier, Frenchman and widower, resided in the same area as above.

Louis Fortin, Frenchman, wed to Manuella Aragon, Spanish, resided on land of Francois Prudhomme which was among the Adais Indians, at Los Adais.

Francisco Prudhomme, Frenchman wed to Anne Marie Rambin, Frenchwoman, two sons and seven daughters. Prudhomme in 1805 was 74 years old. This land among the Adais Indians was granted to Prudhomme by DeMezieres in 1771. Francois Prudhomme was a trader among the Indians and at the same time had a Spanish co-partner, Antonio Gil y Barbo, who traded among the Spanish along El Camino Real. Manuel Flores was another partner of Prudhomme, also Miguel Viciente who later sold his grant to Isaac Crow. It is very likely that Viciente at his out of the way home on Sabine River was a trader in contraband merchandise supplied by Prudhomme. The trail leading from Sabine River and the home of Miguel Viciente on Bayou San Patrice and eastward to the Red River via Converse, Pleasant Hill and to Bayou Pierre was a contraband trail. In 1723 Paul Muller established Post du Bayou Pierre, with contraband trade with the Spanish as his aim. Post du Bayou

Pierre developed into the Town of Bayou Pierre. This trail was traveled by Gutierrez and his followers when they were pursued by the Royalists, Spanish Troops. Post du Bayou Pierre, The Town of Bayou Pierre, King Hill and Jordan Ferry are all one and the same.

Pierre Dole (Pedro Dolet or Peter Dolet), Frenchman mentioned earlier wed Dona Rose Duprez, Spanish woman, resided on Bayou Adais (Winn Creek, west of Robeline, Louisiana).

Andria Valentine (Andria Balentine) Frenchman, wed Angela Molis, French woman, resided on Bayou La Jeune (Youngs' Bayou) near Coldwater vicinity.

Elina Wales, widow, American, three sons, Jacob, Thomas and Benjamin, resided on Bayou La Jeune.

Jacinto Gane (Jacinto Gannie, Gainnie, Gagnier), evidently a son of Pierre Gainnie, resided on land grant mentioned before.

Bacitio Gane of the same family mentioned above, Frenchman, wed Marie Lafita, Spanish woman.

Miguel Viciente, Spanish, mentioned before, wed Elena Roubeaux French woman, is the same land grant sold to Isaac Crow, which was being claimed by his son, Michel.

Pedro Roblo, Pierre Roubeaux, Frenchman, wed Magdelina Baptiste, Spanish woman, resided on Durango Creek.

Francisco Moran, Frenchman, wed Anna Maria, an Apache mestizo, the word *mestizo* in Spanish refers to a half-breed offspring of Spanish and Indian parents. Moran was an Indian trader for Anthanaze De Mezieres and operated along El Camino Real with a certified passport. He was said to speak French, Spanish and thirty-eight Indian dialects. He often accompanied DeMezieres as an interpreter. He asked for and received three acres of land on El Camino Real in the vicinity of Robeline, Louisiana. In 1805 Moran was seventy-eight years old.

Santiago Christine, Frenchman wed Marie D'Ortigeaux, French woman, resided on Bayou Pierre.

Antonio Rocquier, Frenchman, wed Marrianne, an English woman. This grant by De Mezieres has already been mentioned as to location.

Michel Crow, Englishman, wed Margarita La Fleur (LaFleur-Flores) Spanish woman, resided, as before mentioned in the claim of the firm, Murphy, Smith, Barr and Davenport.

In 1806 the following had applied for homesteads and received quarter sections of land: William Eldridge, George Mac Tier, Manuel Flores, John Cartez, Asa Becherson, Stephen Wallace and Seaborne Maillard.

Peter Belieu, who had been living on Bayou Pierre for fifty years, declared squatters' rights, as did Walter Weathersby, Francois Dubois, David Chase, Jean Pierre Grappe, Joseph Teanriz, Mickel Chasneau, Benjamin Boullett, William Cockerville, Denise Dies (Diez).

In the area of Cypress, Flora Provincal and Kisatchie, Louisiana, the land was granted by Athanase De Mezieres in 1771-1776, to: Pierre Joseph Maises, at Cypress, Louisiana, on Lago Acasse; Baptiste Prudhomme, also near Cypress; Madam Marie Palagie on Drunkard's Bayou near Flora, Louisiana; Thomas Vascoque near Provincal, Louisiana; Joseph Procell, a Spaniard, west of Bayou Derbonne, west of Melrose, Louisiana; Pierre Sanscalier on Bayou Kisatchie near Kisatchie, Louisiana, who used the fresh spring water of Kisatchie and made the finest corn whiskey on the whole Neutral Strip; and, Leander Lasso on Petite Bayou Pierre, south and west of present-day Cloutierville, Louisiana.

Within the area of present day Sabine Parish were these settlers in 1805: Joe Leaky, John Wadell, Christopher Anthony, Thomas Hicks, Jacob Winfree, Jose Rivers, Peter Patterson, David Weathersby, David Walters, John Gordon, Benjamin Winfree, James Kirklin, Andres Galinto, Jose Procell, James Denny, Manuel Bustamento, John Yocum, Jessy Yocum and Michel Crow. E. Dillon, A. Davidson, Barbe, Beebe, Cartinez, Slocomb and Addington.

FAMILY TREE OF ST. DENIS

(Born Sept. 17, 1676, Died June 11, 1744.)

Jean Juchereau wed Marie Langlois.

Son

Nicholas Juchereau de St. Denis wed Theresa Giffard.

Son

Louis Juchereau de St. Denis wed Emanuello Sanchez de Navarro Ramone.

Children were:

Marie Rose Juchereau De St. Denis wed Jacques De La Chaise.

Louis Charles Juchereau de St. Denis wed Marie Barbier.

Marie des Delores Simone de St. Denis wed Cesair de Blanc.
Child, Louis Charles de Blanc.

Louise Margarite Juchereau de St. Denis. — Died young.

Marie Patronille Feliciane Juchereau de St. Denis wed Athanase DeMezieres. There was one child, Louise Feliciane DeMezieres, who may have wed a Prudhomme.* DeMezieres' second wife was Pelagie Fazenda, whose name is noted on several birth records as a Godmother.

Marie des Neiges Juchereau de St. Denis wed Manuell Antoine de Soto Bermuda.

Children were:

Marie Manuello de Soto wed Augustain Le Noir.

Ludoric Joseph Firmin de Soto.

Marie Joseph de Soto—died young.

Joseph Marcel de Soto wed Marie Ballio.

S. Antoine Gertrudes de Soto wed Manuell Flores.

Emanuello Marie Anne de Soto wed Joseph Rambin.

---

*Pierre Subastion Prudhomme.

BAPTISMAL RECORDS OF NATCHITOCHES
1734 TO 1740

Child	Parents	Godfather (Parin)	Godmother (Marin)
J. Avanboite.	J. Avanboite. Marie Badin.	Francois Godeau.	Rose De St. Denis.
1735			
J. Dupree.	J. Dupree. Anna Maria Phillipo.	J. Dupree.	L. Riotou.
H. Triche.	J. Triche. Lorette Grenot.	A. Gonzales.	E. S. De Navarre (Madam St. Denis)
Neona Bautimino.	L. Bautimino. Theresa Navarre	L. J. De St. Denis. (Louis Jauchero)	E. S. De St. Denis. (Madam St. Denis)
A. Lage.	A. Lage. Maria De La Chase.	A. Dupin.	Anna Verger.
A. Prevot.	Nicholas Prevot. Yevonne Dubois.	J. Bossier.	Ananise Chaneau. (Madame Chmard)
J. Leroy.	Lise Francis Gillot. Silveran LeRoy.	M. de St. Denis.	Madam de St. Denis.
J. Rachal.	Pierre Rachal. Marie Anna Benoist.	P. Cussin.	Jeanne Piquerey.
1736			
M. V. Prudhomme.	J. B. Prudhomme. Celest Mestier.	G. Chevert.	Marie Victoria-Gonzalez Derbonne.
Theresa Levasseur.	J. Lavasseur. M. F. Bourdon.	G. Chevert.	Theresa Barbier.
J. B. Brevel.	J. B. Brevel. A. Tvianac.	J. B. Prudhomme.	Marcel Bacques.
M. Chevert.	G. Chevert Y. Mestier.	J. B. Prudhomme.	Marainne Bacques.
R. Dupree.	J. Dupree. Theresa Barbier. (Second wife of Dupree).	Rime Avare.	H'Elane Dubois.

Ann Lage.
M. F. Gauthier.
M. L. Manne.
N. Prevot.

R. Possoit.
M. R. Boisselier.
L. Rondin.
C. F. Lavasseur.
M. F. Chevert.
J. B. Trichelle.

H. M. S. Brevel.
J. B. Prudhomme.
J. Rachal.
F. Rambin.
E. Verger.

Justine Lage.
F. Buart.
J. Gauthier.
Manuello Lorenzo Devaca.
Francisci Manne.
Joan Derbonne.
Nicholas Prevot.
Yevonne Dubois.

R Possiot.
A. M. Phillipi.
J. Boisselier.
C. Labarre.
J. Rondin.
E. Flores.
J. Lavesseur.
M. F. Bourdon.
G. Chavert.
Th Barbier.
L. Trichell.
M. Demonde.

J. B. Brevel.
A. Tvianac.
J. B. Prudhomme.
Celest Mestier.
P. Rachal.
M. A. Benoist.
Andres Rambin.
Zelia Prevot.
J. Verger.
A. Demont.
J. Lager.

1737
A. Lage.
R. Dubois.
J. B. Derbonne.
P. Prevot.

1738
H. Riche.
J. McCartey.
Luis Goudeau (Doctor)
F. Manne.
G. Barbier.
J. B. Derbonne.

1739
L. Goudeau.
F. Daicdeau.
J. Rondin.
Louis Rambin. (Grandfather also)
L. DeMalathe.
L. DeMalathe.

M. de La Chase.
Marie Francine Renaudier.
Marie Gonzales Derboune.
Zelia Prevot.

A. Dumont.
E Santhez Y Navarre.
J. Piguery.
J. U. Garcia.
M. F. Bourdon.
A. DeManche.

J. Piguery.
Donna Girtrudus Gonzalez.
E. Rachal.
Marie Cathern de Poutree (Grandmother)
M. A. Rousseau.
M. Flores.

Child	Parents	Godfather (Parin)	Godmother (Marin)
L. Lager.	F. Buard.	Manuel Flores.	Th. Flores.
L. DeMatlathe.	L. DeMatalathe.		
E. Trechelle.	M. Flores. H. Trichell.	L. J. de St. Denis.	E Sanchez de St. Deni.
E. Possiot.	M. Charles. R. Possiot.	S. J. Maderne.	M. Buard.
P. DeLuche. M. DeLuche.	A. M. Phillipi. J. DeLuche. M. Benoist.* (Melanie Benoist)	P. Fausse.	J. Grenot.

Note: the above is that of the Justine deLuche Family. The Child P. DeDuche being named Pierre after Pierre Fausse who was the Godfather and perhaps also the Grandfather.

M. LeRoy.	Siveran LeRoy. Lise Francis Guillot.	G. Bosseau.	M. de La Chais

1740

A. Prudhomme.	J. Prudhomme. C. Mestier.	L. J. de St. Denis.	Donna E. Sanchez- de St. Denis.
H. D. Marine.	J. A. Marine. G. O. L. Perot.	H. Trechelle.	M. Dumont.
E. Vidol.	E. Vidol. C. Lavespere.	J. DeLuche.	M. Benoist De Luche.
H. L. Lavespere.	H. Lavespere. C. Brossilier.	L. J. de St. Denis.	M. Derbonne.
M. Leroy.	Siveran LeRoy L. S. Guillot.	J. Deluche.	M. H. Guillot.

Note: Margarite LeRoy who was Christened in 1739 wed Louis Rachall, a French Soldier, in 1757. She was 17 years old. Her Sister Marie who was Christened in 1740 wed Jean Baptiste Le Campti who was also a French Soldier, in 1758.

M. J. Levasseur.	J. Lavasseur. M. F. Bourdon.	J. B. Derbonne.	M. V. Gonzalez.
C. Hernandez.	G. Hernandez. J. Renaudier.	P. Renaudier.	M. F. Renaudier.
M. F. Possiot.	R. Possiot. A. M. Phillippi.	L. J. de St. Denis.	M. Sanchez.

SOLDIERS IN NATCHITOCHES — 1742

Louis Juchereau De St. Denis, Commandante.

Captains: Cesar De Blanc also a son-in-law of St. Denis. Cesar Borme, Jean Gainard, Baltazar Villars and Louis Pablo Villenfev.

Lieutenants: Jacques De La Chase, Bernardo Dortolen, (Dortigeux), Jacques Terpeux, Vincent Perrier, Jean Baptiste Derbonne, and Jean Baptiste De Duc, Anthanase DeMezieres and Philippe Coubiere.

Sergeants: Gurelleon Lavespere, Michael Gallion, Joseph Lattier, Joseph Trichell (Trichel), Nicholas Tournier, *Guiellerno Lestage*, Alexis Grappe, Remi Possiot, Louis Possiot, Bartholme Rachal and Angelus Challettre (Schellette — Chellette—Schellet) Alarge Chabineux.

Corporals: Antonio Le Noir, Jean Dubois, Antonio Distin, Jean Dupuy, Allarge Dupuy, Nicholas Pent, Christopher Perault, Felix Jeanot and Olivere Fredieu and Entoine Desadier.

Musketeers: Louis Moinet, Francois Hugue, Bartholme Monpierre, Andries Compiere, Pierre Renaudiere, Luis Antee (also Town Crier), Regimigo Tontin, Marino de Muy, Domingo St. Primo, Everiste Possiot, Gaspard Toil, Antonio de St. Denis, Louis Bertrand, Jean Prudhomme, Henri Barbarousse, Louis Pierre La Cour, Armand Beaudoin, Pierre Baillio and Jean and Nicholas Layssard (brothers who were the sons of Antoin Nicholas Layssard who in 1723 established "Post Du Rapides" The town of Colfax Louisiana is on the Land Grant of Jean and Nicholas Layssard who had established a trading post in that area in 1747), Siveran Le Roy, Francois Beaudoin and Andries La Cour.

MERCHANTS, FARMERS AND TRADERS
IN NATCHITOCHES — 1742

TRADERS

Pierre Bisson, Joseph Blancpain, Jean Basquet, Pierre Blot, Jean Chapuis (Traded as far west as New Mexico, Jean Chapuis Jr., the son, later became known as the Father of Oklahoma he developed the largest chain of Trading Posts which was never equalled. The territory covered the Missouri River Area, the upper Red River Area and as far west as the Colorado River). Pierre Gaignee (Gainnie) (Gane) (Gainiee) (Gaignie) had a trading post on Bon Dieu Falls which was at that time on Rigilet de Bon Dieu was later called Creola Landing and now Montgomery, La.

MERCHANTS

Sieur Barme, Nicholas Fazinda, Antoin Rambin (Tailor Shop), Louis Lemee, Estabin Pavie, Dominec Mancheca (Tavern Owner), Michel de Chasne, Louis Bonnafons, Luis Caesar Barme, Mathais La Courte, and Pierre Joans.

HORSE TRADERS

Nicholas Chef, Nicholas La Mathie, Brognard, D'Autherive, Duviviere, DuBuche and Pierre DuPain.

FARMERS

Jacques Bacquet, Ezeb Mercer, Charles de Blanc, Gailier Gallion, and Jean Baptiste Brevel. And Soldier-Farmer, Pierre Brosset.

SOLDIER FARMERS

Bartholme Charbonet, Louis Moinet, Andries La Cour, Bernardo Dartigo, Jean Baptiste Derbonne, Guiellerno Lestage, Remi Poissoit, Angelus Chellettree, Joseph Lattier and Alexis Grappe.

Priests at Nachitoches were Father Vitree and Dagobare.

MERCHANTS AT LOS ADAIS

Antonio Flores, Edwardo Nugent, Jose LaLima, Luis De Qundise and Joseph Antonio Bonetis.

SOLDIERS AT LOS ADAIS — 1742

Jose Maria Gonzalez, Captain and Commandante second to Governor.

Captain Eucibia Luis Cazrola.

Lieutenants: Bernardo Dortolan, Franciscio Garcia and Ensigne, Jauquine Cardova.

Soldiers: Jose Duprez, Hortego Cardova, Geronimo Gallardo, Thoribolo de La Fuentes, Fernando Rodriguez, Franciscio Uque, Antonio y Barbo (Father of Gil Y Barbo), Luis Garcia, Antonio Barbarjo De Vargez, Estaban Bonites, Elonzo Bustimento, Pedro Chacon, Greganzoto Martinez, Surrento Flores, Felix Solis, Luis Solis and Phillippe Hernandex.

FARMERS

Durango Y Oconna, (Ocon) Sanchez, Alberto Cartinez, Jose Guierre, Manuello Flores, Gregory Procell and Salvadore Bano, Sanchez, Juan De More, Pedro Pasquell, Gaspardo Conterio, Patrice Lopez, Cadet Toro, Mechell La Rouex and Antonie Sepulvado.

REFERENCES

Baptismals and Death Registers, 1704-1740, Cathedral Archives, Mobile, Alabama.

Concessions, Louisiana Historical Society Library, Tulane Library, New Orleans. Transcripts.

French MSS., Mississippi Valley, 1676-1869, Louisiana Historical Society Library, Tulane Library, New Orleans.

Notes and Docquements Historiques de la Louisiane, Tulane Library, New Orleans.

Hennepin, Louis A., *Description of Louisiana,* Paris 1683, edited and translated by J. G. Shea, New York 1880.

Joutel, *A journal of the last voyage performed by Monsr. De la Salle* to the Gulf of Mexico to find the Mouth of the Mississippi River, Written in French by M. Joutel, a commander in the expedition. Caxton Club, London, 1896.

Kelerec, *Report of 1758,* New Orleans Library.

LePage du Pratz, *Historie de la Louisiane,* 3 vols Paris, 1758.

The Jesuit Relations and Allied Documents, edited by R. G. Thwaites, 71 vols, Cleveland 1896-1901.

Colonial Records of North Carolina, edited by William L. Saunders, 10 vols, Raleigh, N. C. 1896-1901.

La Harpe, Bernard de, *Journal Historique de l'Establissement des Francais a la Louisiane*, Nouvelle-Orleans 1831. New Orleans Library.

Le Gac, Charles (Director of the Company of the Indies) *Memorie d'apris les Voyages sur la Louisiana*, la Geographie, La situation de la Colonie Francois ou 25 Anust 1718 au 5 Mars 1721 et des moynesd de l'ameliorer, 1722. Boston Public Library.

Blanchard, Rufus, *History of Illinois*, Chicago 1883.

Breese, Sidney, *The early history of Illinois*, from its Discovery by the French, in 1673, until its concession to Great Britain in 1763, including the Narration of Marquette's Discovery of the Mississippi, Chicago, 1884.

Bunner, E., *History of Louisiana from its first discovery and settlement to the present time*, New York 1841.

Bureau of American Ethnology, Bulletin 43, *Indian Tribes of the Lower Mississippi Valley* Adjacent to the Coast of the Gulf of Mexico, Washington 1911.

Speed, Thomas, *The Wilderness Road*. A description of the route of travel by which the pioneers and early settlers first came to Kentucky. In Filson Club Publication, No. 2, Louisville, Kentucky. 1886.

Thwaites, Ruben Gold, Wisconsin, *The Americanization of the French Settlements, American Commonwealths*, Boston and New York, 1908.

B. F. French, Editor, *Historical Collections of Louisiana*, 5 parts, New York 1869-1875.

B. F. French, *Historical Collections of Louisiana and Florida*, New Series, 2 vols 1869-1875.

Gayarre, Charles, *History of Louisiana*, The French Dominion, 4 vols, New Orleans, 1885.

Gayarre, Charles, *Historie de la Louisiane*, 2 vols, Nouvelle Orleans 1846-1847.

Gayarre, Charles, *Louisiana, Its History as a French Colony*, New York, 1852.

Hienrich, Pierre, *La Louisiane sous la Compaignie des Indies*, 1717-1731.

Louisiana Conservationist, January 1957, A map drawn by Simon Le Page du Pratz of the Lower Mississippi Valley, showing the location of numerous Indian Tribes.

Delisle's *Map, 1718*, New York Public Library.

Fleur de Lys and Calumet, by Richebourg Gaillard McWilliams.

Analysis of Indian Village Sites from Louisiana and Mississippi. Anthropological Study No. 2. By John A. Ford.

Cavalier in the Wilderness. By Ross Phares.

Alexandria and Qld Red River Country, by Harry and Elizabeth Eskew.

A History of the Red River Watershed, by J. Fair Hardin.

Northwestern Louisiana, by J. Fair Hardin.

History of Sabine Parish, by John G. Belisle, Many, Louisiana, 1912.

History of Louisiana, by Alcee Fortier, 4 vols.

A History of Louisiana, by Charles Gayarre, 4 vols.

History of Natchitoches, Louisiana, by Milton Dunn (Louisiana Historical Quarterly, 111 (January 1920) Pages 26-56).

Our Catholic Heritage in Texas, by Carlos E. Castaneda, 7 vols.

French Civilization and Culture in Natchitoches (Peabody College Bulletin No. 310 Nashville 1941) by Portre-Bobinski.

Natchitoches the Up-to-Date Oldest Town in Louisiana, by Clara Mildred Smith and Portre Bobinski, New Orleans 1936.

Natchitoches, Oldest Settlement in the Louisiana Purchase, published by The Association of Natchitoches Women, 1958. Printed by the Natchitoches Times.

Ride the Red Earth, by Paul I. Wellman.

A History of Louisiana, by Elizabeth Grace King and J. R. Ficklen.

Commerce of Louisiana During the French Regime by Surry.

History of the Caddo Indians. A Thesis by William B. Glover of the University of Texas 1932.

The History of Louisiana Agriculture, by Williamson.

Historical and Biographical Notes by B. F. French. Published by J. Sabine 1869.

Pichardo's Limits of Louisiana and Texas. 4 vols by Charles W. Hackett. Published by the University of Texas Press 1941.

Louisiana and Florida by B. F. French.

Discovery and Explorations of the Missisisppi, by John G. Shea, Published by Clinton Hall, New York City, 1852.

Source Material on the *History and Ethnology of the Caddo Indians,* Louisiana State University Press.

Mississippi Provincal Archives, 3 vols French Dominion by Albelt Godfrey Sanders, M.A., Millsaps College, published Jackson, Mississippi, Department of Archives of History 1932.

Athanase DeMezieres Books 1 and 2 of the *Louisiana and Texas Frontier 1768 to 1780.* By Herbert Eugene Bolton. Published by The Authur H. Clark Co., Cleveland, 1914.

The Sword was their Passport, by Harris Gaylord Warren. Published by the Louisiana State University Press. Baton Rouge, La. 1943.

PERSONALITIES

(The names with stars are descended from early ancestors mentioned in the text or listed in the early records of El Camino Real area)

Here are some short biographies of individuals who have each in his or her own way contributed to the progress of our El Camino Real upper territory.

Many of them are descendants of the earliest settlers, and their families have been in Louisiana for nearly 250 years. Very few in Louisiana can claim such distinction, for even the founders of New Orleans came later.

The families of others written about here settled in this area years afterward, some in modern times. But they have adopted the land as their own an are just as proud of its history and traditions as the "old timers."

All have, by living up to the standard of older days, added to the well being of the community and improved it socially, economically and politically. They have made it attractive to tourists and visitors, and new permanent residents find it a most attractive place in which to live. The people of today who live along El Camino Real are worthy of their sires.

CLIFTON ROBERT AMMONS

Clifton Robert Ammons of Many, La., wed Ethel Jeanne Matherne of Houma, La. Their children are: Robert Dale, L.S.U.; Dianna Drew, Centenary College; Kenneth Ellis, Larry Wayne and Suzanne Jeanne. Mr. Ammons truly exemplifies our modern-day citizen of the El Camino Real area. He is a Farmer and Stockman, a School teacher and State Representative of Sabine Parish. The Toledo Bend Dam, one of his pet projects, shall some day prove its value to this Louisiana and Texas area. Mr. Ammons' work with the F.F.A. is second to none other in the State. He is truly an excellent community worker.

BERNICE C. ARTHUR

Bernice C. Arthur, owner of the Many Insurance Agency, wed Miss Helen E. Fuglaar of Alexandria, La. Their children are Thomas C. and James R.. Mr. Arthur is a descendant of the families Roberds and Dollarhide who had settled near Sabine Town in 1829. Camp Sabine, Sabine Town and Sabine Blockhouse were one and the same—Camp Sabine established by Gen. Wilkinson in 1811, Sabine town by the settlers and Sabine Blockhouse by Gen. Gaines in 1828.

JOHN MILTON BELISLE

John Milton Belisle for 30 years was editor and publisher of the Sabine Index at Many, La. He was a member of the Town Council for 4 years, Mayor of Many for 16 years and State Representative for 8 years. He was the son of John Graves Belisle who wrote the first History of Sabine Parish. John Milton wed Alice Wagley of Many. Their daughter, Hanna Jane, wed W. Carlie Brumfield. Their children are Alicia and Juliannah.

JACK AND ALBERT BELL

Jack and Albert Bell own and manage the Bell Brothers General Store at the corner of Texas and Clark Streets in Robeline, La. This business location is on what was at one time the Joe Robeline farm which pre-dates the founding of Robeline, La. Joe Robeline had a Way-Station at this location during the Neutral Strip period.

Jack Bell wed Carolyne Elizabeth Powell of Pleasant Hill, La. Their children are Roy Patrick and Don Gregory. Mrs. Jack Bell is a teacher at the Robeline Elementary School.

Albert Bell wed Mildred Marie Tooke of Homer, La. They have one child, Judieth Carrol. Mrs. Albert Bell is the Home Economics Teacher at the Robeline High School.

LLOYD VERNON BLUNT

Lloyd Vernon Blunt wed Miss Lynn L. Haynes. They own and operate the L&L Cafe in Many, La., which is located on the main street of Many. This street is a portion of El Camino Real. Their children are: Mary Joan who wed Harold Lloyd Southards, and Lloyd Wallace who is in the U. S. Marines. Mr. Blunt is a Marine veteran of the Nicaraguan campaign. Mr. and Mrs. Blunt are natives of Virginia and have become a very definite asset to the El Camino Real area of Many, La.

SIDNEY WILLIAMS BRIGHT

Sidney Williams Bright, Co-owner of Bright and Son Laundry and Cleaners at 224 Amulet St. in Natchitoches, La., wed Beatrice Williams of Bronson, Tex. Their children are: Sidney Williams, Jr., who wed Etheline St. Andre (their children are Elizabeth Ann, Rhonda Jean and Sarah Lou) ; Mary Francis Bright wed Stephen Melou Brown, Jr. (their children are Stephen Melou III, Cheryl Anne and William Dudley). Mr. Bright, Sr., originally was a native of Hemphill, Tex., where he was at one time Clerk of Court for Sabine County.

JOSEPH FREDERICK BROSSET★

Joseph Frederick Brosset, Overseer on the Bayou Camite Plantation at Derry, La., wed Eva Moreau. Their children are (a) Mary Jo, wed to Doctor Elwin Adams of Belmont, La.; (b) Lester Roy, Lt., U. S. Army; (c) Billy Jean, wed Lawrence M. Carnahan, Jr.

MRS. ELI HOUSTON BUTTS★

Mrs. Eli Houston Butts, neé Eleanor Irene Lovell, route 2, Colfax, La., is a typest, clerk and saleswoman for Blair Products. Children are Bonnie Lynn and Marilyn Louise. Mrs. Butts is a descendant through the Baillio Chellettre family to Jean Layssard, who was a son of Etoinne Layssard who established Post Du Rapides in 1723, the beginning of Alexandria, La. The present Town of Colfax, La., is on the French land grant of Jean Nicholas Layssard.

JAMES COCO

James Coco, Mortician and manager of the First National Funeral Home at Natchitoches, La. He wed Clara Belle Stringer of Midland, Texas. Their children are: James Gary, Lucy Dolores, Charles Anthony and Elizabeth Anne.

Mr. Coco is a son of Albert F. Coco and Rhoda Escude.

Albert F. Coco is a descendant of Dominic Baldonide who came to America with Lafayette to fight with the American Revolutionary Army. After the Revolution he migrated to Pointe Coupee, La. and from there to the Alexandria area near Marksville, La.

There are several versions of how the name Baldonide changed to Coco. This is not unusual in this section of Louisiana. For example: LeBrun, nickname for Jean Bossier; Duprez, nickname for Francois Dion Derbonne; and Dauphine, nickname for Charles Bertrand.

These above three nicknames are now family names in the central Louisiana area.

Fred Litton Cooper
Mrs. Dottie Dee Cooper

Fred Litton Cooper, owner of Cooper's Pharmacy at Robeline, Louisiana, wed Miss Dottie Dee Scarborough. There are two children: Norman Otto who married Doris Jordan of Robeline, and Margaret Sue who wed Aubry Ralph Barnette of Robeline. Mr. Cooper is by far the leading historian of the Robeline area. He and Mrs. Cooper have kept alive the value of Robeline historywise. Cooper's Pharmacy is a must-stop for all tourists who travel into Robeline.

Mrs. Dottie Dee Cooper is a member of the N W P H N (Association of Natchitoches Women for the Preservation of Historic Natchitoches). She has taken upon herself to be the Official Greeter for tourists who visit this section.

In relating the history of the Robeline vicinity Mrs. Cooper has the statements of these historians to refer to: John Belisle's History of Sabine Parish as well as earlier authorities.

Cabeza De Vaca in his book written in 1540, declares that he was among the Adais Indians in 1530. De Vaca, a survivor of the Panfillio Narvez expedition into Florida in 1528. De Vaca spelled the name Adais. (Atyas) exactly as later Spaniards spelled the name.

B. F. French in his interpretations of early Spanish documents, placed the Hernando De Soto expedition among the Adais Indians. French translated the writings of Gonzado Quadrado Charmillio who was the Chronnicalor for the De Soto expedition. Charmillio wrote: "This Wednesday, March 21, 1540 we came to a place called Toalli."

Lloyd Earl Dean

Lloyd Earl Dean, Stockman, Planter and Co-owner of the Boyce Gin Co., at Boyce, La. Mr. Dean resides on the Dean Plantation south of Colfax, La. He wed Sarah Florence Beall of Pineville,

La. Their children are Sarah Frances, William Burkett, George Carlton and Albert Lloyd.

Mr. Dean is a son of Garland Carlton Dean and Leona Creed. Garland Carlton Dean is a son of Albert Allen Dean and Clara Price. Albert Allen Dean founded Fairmount Landing on the Red River between Colfax and Boyce. Shipping ledgers now in the possession of Lloyd Earl Dean show that the Fairmount Landind did business with the Steamboats *Garland, Valley Queen, Laura Lee, Keokuk, Peninah, Halliette, Jesse K. Bell, G. W. Sutree, Decotah, E. B. Wheelock, The John D. Scully* and the *Nat F. Dortch.* With Steamboat Captains John J. Dodd, F. T. Aucoin, H. J. Brinker, G. Scully, S. J. Bozaman, A. G. White, William Gillin and James T. O'Rey.

Albert Allen Dean was the steamboat agent for the Red River and Coastline Steamship Co., The Red River Packet Co., and the T&P Railway Company which had the Steamboats *E. B. Wheelock* and the *C. W. Sutterlee.*

Lloyd Earl Dean traces his ancestry to Abraham Alexander who signed the "Mecklinburg Declaration" of North Carolina just prior to the Declaration of Independence.

The Dean family dates back to 1608, the birth date of Nathanial Dean who came to America on the ship *Paul* in 1635.

ALVIN J. DeBlieux, Sr.★

Alvin J. DeBlieux, Sr., owner of the New Drug Store at corner of St. Denis and Second Sts., and DeBlieux's Drug in Broadmore Shopping Center, wed Miss Anette Block of Bunkie, La. Their children are Alvin, Jr. and Margaret Ann who wed Robert Ross Anderson of Chicago, Ill. Mr. DeBlieux is a fifth generation Natchitochan. His great-great grandfather settled land on the east bank of Red River opposite the Bluffs at Grand Ecore, La.

JACK LESTAN DeBlieux★

Jack Lestan DeBlieux, Planter, Stockman and Agent 1 of the Enforcement Division of the Department of Wildlife and Fisheries, wed Eloise Adkins of Coushatta, La. Their children are: Freddy,

Barry Freeman, Molly Darla and Dan David. The Gaines Military Road from Fort Jesup to Arkansas borders the DeBlieux property. The River-crossing was just arear of the DeBlieux residence. Jack Lestan's ancestors saw the coming of Yankee Gunboats up the Red River.

MRS. LAWRENCE CLEVELAND DELATIN★

Mrs. Lawrence Cleveland DeLatin, neé Florence Adeline Case, owns and manager Florence's Beauty Shop at 575 West Main Street, Many, La. She was born in Palatka, Florida. Mr. DeLatin is a descendant of Durango y Oconna (Ocon), who, after having served his required tenure as a Spanish soldier, acquired and settled land in the Robeline area. There are many descendants today branching from Durango Oconna.

MRS. PERCY ROBERTS DILLON★

Mrs. Percy Roberts Dillon, neé Caroline Eloise Brook. From her marriage are these children: Percy Roberts, Jr., wed Kathleen Lambert, their son is Michael John; and Rilla Diana wed Garland Carlton.

Mrs. Percy Roberts Dillon is a Beautitian and owns and manages the Petite Beauty Shoppe at 435 San Antonio St., which is a portion of El Camino Real and is the Main Street in Many, Louisiana.

MRS. HERBERT DORFER, PH.★

Mrs. Herbert Dorfer, Ph., neé Ada Trichel of Fairview Alpha, La., taught school in Natchitoches Parish for 25 years before studying and becoming a pharmacist. Her business establishment, Campti Drug Store, is on Edenborne Street. Her children by her first marriage are Blanche McElwee, who wed Dr. A. L. Hushey of Opelika, Ala., and Ray McElwee who wed Rosemary Peters of Austin, Texas.

Edenborne Street in Campti, La., is named for a famous steamboat captain.

Exchange Bank & Trust Co.

The Exchange Bank and Trust Co., at the corner of Front and St. Denis Streets in Natchitoches, La., will have at this printing ended its 70th year of continuous service in Natchitoches. This bank at its beginning occupied two other locations on Front St., and in September 1892 the Exchange Bank erected and moved into the building which is the present location of the bank. In the span of 70 years of service there have only been four Presidents: Dr. J. W. Cockerham, J. Henry Williams, Arthur C. Watson and at present Mr. Harold Kaffie. In 1826 this street corner was called "Lescal's Corner" because of Lescal's Dance Hall and Theater. This theater thrilled the local citizens with such plays as: Romeo and Juliet, Macbeth, and Bewick and Graham.

Ambrose Charles Flores★

Ambrose Charles Flores wed Dovie Lea Frye of Minden, La. Their daughter, Dolores Ann, wed Aubrey Randall Word and they reside in Shreveport. The Flores family has been connected with the El Camino Real from the very beginning of its occupancy by the Spanish. There were very few expeditions from Mexico City which did not contain a Flores as a member. Ambrose represents the 10th generation of Flores in the Robeline area.

C. B. Funderburk

C. B. Funderburk is owner and manager of the Starlite Motel, Highway 171 south, Many, La. He wed Miss Mahalia Eunice Johnson of Chopin, La. Their children are: Jacquelyn, who wed Guy Cheek; Jeryl D., who wed Suzane Chaput of Portland, Maine; Larry Don, who attends Many High School; and Mary Jane, who attends Many elementary school. C. B. is a fifth generation descendant of A. Taylor who settled near Kisatchie, La., in the Neutral Strip.

Mr. and Mrs. Clive Glover

Miss Estelle McLean of Goldonna, La., wed Clive Glover of Natchitoches, La. Mrs. Glover owns and manages Glover's Gift Shop

— 157 —

which is located on the south end of Front Street, the oldest street in the original Louisiana Purchase, at 459 Jefferson and Front Streets. Mr. Glover is a Master Plumber and contractor. He is a descendant of Colonel Caspari, who when a State Representative acquired and established Northwestern State College. He built the Tap — a railroad from Natchitoches to Cypress, La.

JOSEPH JESSE GRAPPE★

Joseph Jesse Grappe, owner of Value Pak Grocer at 1200 Washington St., wed Exie Borland of Dodson, La. Their children are Bennie Evon, wed to Robert Wayne Womack; Robbie Jean, and Shirley Ann, who wed James Buckley. Mr. Grappe, a descendant of Pierre Batiste Grappe, who was a French soldier at Natchitoches in 1741. Jesse represents the eighth generation of Grappes in the Natchitoches area. Fishing is his favorite sport.

HON. LLOYD JAMES HARRISON★

Lloyd James Harrison, Mayor of Montgomery, La., a merchant and planter and a historian in his own right, wed to Miss Gussie Teddlie. He is a descendant of Mrs. T. O. Harrison, who when the Yankee gunboats were firing on Creola Landing, walked out on her porch and waved an apron. Admiral Porter, admiring such bravery, ordered the cease-fire signal to be given.

LOYD BERNARD HARRISON

Loyd Bernard Harrison, Science-Agri. instructor at Colfax High School, wed Doris Olene Jones. Their children are: Loyd Bernard, Jr., Janis Cay, Melvin Lee and Connie Suse. Mr. Harrison is also a Planter and Stockman as were his ancestors. He is a descendant of the Harrisons who were very active in the readjustment period after the Civil War. At that time the town of Montgomery was known as Creola Bluff Landing on Red River. Many of the fine families of this section of Grant Parish are descendants of those inhabitants of Creola Landing.

THOMAS JAMES HARRISON★

Thomas James Harrison, Gen. Manager of the W. T. McCain

Consignee Distributor of Esso Products at Montgomery, La., wed Marion Blanche Wood of Mansfield, La. Their children are: Tommy Rey, Ronnie Lee, Johnnie Payne and Donnie Wayne. He is a 5th generation descendant of Thomas J. Harrison, Capt. 3rd Inf. Reg., which was stationed at Fort Jesup.

THOMAS ORTENBURGER HARRISON★

Thomas Ortenburger Harrison, barber of Montgomery, La., wed Mabel Clair Fletcher. Their children are: Margie Dorothy, librarian, and Thomas O., Jr. who wed Paula Gilbert of Minden, La. Their child, Jennifer Harrison. T. O. Sr. is a barber on Caddo street in Montgomery, and raises fox hounds as a hobby. He is a descendant of Thomas J. Harrison, a signer of the Caddo Indian Treaty, July 1, 1835 who was a captain of the 3rd Inf. of Fort Jesup.

MRS. EARL HERNANDEZ★

Leona Mai Sampite, is a home economics teacher at Cloutierville, La. She wed Earl Hernandez. She is a descendant the Delouche, Guillot, Benoist and Perrier families. Jean Delouche, father of Justine came to Louisiana from LaVendee, France in 1712. By previous marriage Mrs. Hernandez's children are: Joseph Stanley—Louis Henry—and William Rachal, Jr. Joseph wed Doris Ann Brosset: Louis wed Lorinne Bryant and William wed Marcelle Marlick.

EDMOND PRUDHOMME HUGHES★

Edmond Prudhomme Hughes, is the owner and manager of Hughes ready-to-wear, at the corner of Front and Horn streets in Natchitoches, La. He wed Martha Lawton. Their children are: Julie, Martie and Jill. This business location, now famous for the iron lace front and iron spiral stair case in the rear of the building was erected 108 years ago by Gabriel Prudhomme after having assembled the materials in Europe. Natchitochans of a 100 years ago knew this location as "La Mason de Faseion", and it still is that today. Mr. Hughes is a descendant of an early family in this Natchitoches-El Camino Real area.

Mrs. Maxie Mae Jinkins★

Mrs. Maxie Mae Jinkins, neé Maxie Mae Welch of Robeline, La., owns and manages Murphys Cafe at 1215 Washington Street in Natchitchoes, La. She wed Harrison Jinkins and from this union these children:—Mar Jo who wed Hulom Jennings (they have one child, Scott Benjamin)—Judith Charlene—Joseph Andrew—Hannah Maudine—Monita—La Faune—Charles Ray and Wafa Dean.

Mrs. Jinkins is a descendant of Joseph Maxim Welch who maintained a stagecoach station in the Robeline area and who maintained stagecoach service from Natchitoches to Fort Jesup and Baldwin's store. All locations were along El Camino Real. The site of Presidio de Los Adais was owned at one time by this family.

Dr. Edward Everette Jordan★

Edward Everette Jordan, M.D., retired, wed Ruby Dee Burson of Bienville, La. Their children are: Edward Eugene who wed Elaine Hammond (their children are Eugenia and Elizabeth Anne)—Elizabeth Dixon Jordan wed Robert L. Hibbs—Everette Neil Jordan wed Doris Jene Tinsley (their children are Janet and Robert Edward). Doctor Jordan is a descendant of Hanna Dixon and Eugene Erasmus Jordan who helped the wounded soldiers of the Battle of Mansfield. They had settled Jordan Ferry for which this location in now known.

Kaffie & Frederick, Inc.

Kaffie & Frederick, Inc., formerly H. Kaffie and Bros. and S. & H. Kaffie, at 758 and 759 Front street in Natchitoches, La., will in 1963 celebrate their one hundredth anniversary as a firm in business on Front street. The original location was in the vicinity of the Old Darky Statue. It was from this point that the establishment saw the arrival and the retreat of the Union Soldiers after the Battle of Mansfield in 1864. The present building was erected in 1883 by the same firm of contractors who built the old Court House on Second street. At the rear of the present location was a camp ground provided by Kaffie for those who came to Natchitoches to sell their farm produce, and camp-fires burned day and night. The firm of H. Kaffie and Bros. was some 70 years ahead of the modern method of a business establishment providing parking space for its customers.

FRANK MARION KEES, JR.

Frank Marion Kees, Jr. served as Mayor of the City of Natchitoches, La. for twelve consecutive years. He refused to run for the fourth term, deciding instead to become President of Timberline Mfg. Inc. which he was a coorganizer. This manufacturing company is at present producing several designs of chairs. Timberline has again commercialized Natchitoches as did Anthanase DeMezieres 200 years ago when he assigned traders to the different Indian tribes. Following those same Indian trails, which are our State Highways today, the Timberline salesmen have customers in Louisiana, Mississippi, Tennessee, Arkansas, Oklahoma and Texas.

Mr. Kees has served as president of the Central Louisiana Council of Mayors and also the State Municipal Association of Mayors of Louisiana, thus bringing added prestige to our Natchitoches area. How true is this quotation by Mr. Kees: "The rocking chair is the worlds first tranquilizer." Mr. Kees wed Helen Myrtle LeBlanc of Opelousas, La.

MRS. W. M. KNOTT

Much of the credit for the establishment of the Fort Jesup Museum goes to Mrs. W. M. Knott of Many, Louisiana. The building was erected according to the plans of the officers quarters during the time of military occupancy. Mrs. Knott's knowledge of landscaping is seen on the grounds which encompass this building. She is an excellent historian, and was a member of the Research Committee which set the markers for El Camino Real and the Old Natchitoches-to-Natchez Trace. The people of Sabine Parish can well be grateful that they have in their midst such a gifted personality.

LUDDIE LAVESPERE★

Luddie Lavespere, owner and operator of Lavespere's Garage,

Service Station, Grocery and Cafe on Highway 1 at Cloutierville, La. He is the son of Eugene Armours Lavespere and Carline Antee. There is one sister who wed Sullivan LeCaze. Henri Lavespere is listed as an agent of the Company of the West and in association with St. Denis at Natchitoches. Luddie Lavespere represents an 8th generation descendant in the Cloutierville-Natchitoches area.

SAMUEL LeCAZE, SR.★

Samuel LeCaze, Sr., Merchant, Planter, Stockman and Banker of Cloutierville, La. He wed Mazie Vercher. Their children are: Mildred who wed Kenneth David McCoy, their son Kenneth David Jr., Samuel LeCaze, Jr. wed Marie Anita De Louche.
The names LeCaze and Vercher date back to 1728 when these two French soldiers were sent to Post Du Rapides which was the French army post near present Alexandria, La.

SAMUEL LeCAZE, JR.★

Samuel LeCaze, Jr., owner of the LeCaze Estate General Store of Cloutierville, La. He is a successful Merchant, Planter and Stockman. At present he is President of the Natchitoches Parish Fair Association. In 1958 he was chosen Parish Farmer of the Year and placed third among the Louisiana farmers. He was the state's Cattleman father of the year in 1960. Samuel, Jr. wed Marie Anita Delouche. Their children are: Linda Carol, Randall Steven and Tina Jeanine. Mrs. LeCaze is a descendant of Justine Delouche who came to the Cloutierville area in 1735. Samuel is a descendant of the French soldier, LaCaze, of Post Du Rapides of 1728.

HENRY HOWARD LEMOINE★

Henry Howard Lemoine, Planter and Stockman, Route 2 Natchitoches at Clarence, La., wed Iola Jackson of Coushatta, La. Their children are: Linda Gail and Henry Howard, Jr. Both attend St. Mary's School at Natchitoches, La. The Lemoine Family of the Ark.-La.-Tex. area had its beginning with Francois Lemoine

(LeMoyne)—the name being spelled both ways on very early Natchitoches records. This family is that of Iberville and Bienville who were brothers of the LeMoyne family. Francois Lemoine being a nephew, just as was Louis Juchereau De St. Denis whose mother was a LeMoyne or Lemoine. Francois Lemoine is listed as a soldier in Natchitoches in 1723. Thus Henry Howard Lemoine, Sr. represents a 9th generation descendant in our Natchitoches-El Camino Real area.

HENRY OSCAR LESTAGE, JR.★

Henry Oscar Lestage, Jr., member of the law firm of Lestage & Arnette and City Judge of City Court of Jennings, La. Wed to Juliet Xavier Barfield. Their children are: (a) Henry Oscar III wed Anne Scates Warton — one child, Henry Oscar IV. (b) Daniel Barfield, medical student, LSU. (c) David Ramsey, JHS (d) Richard Butler 5th grade. Mr. Lestage's maternal grandmother was Aimie Barberousse. This branch of the family tree dates back to 1713 in the Natchitoches area. A descendant of one of the two Barberousse brothers who were with St. Denis when the Post Des Jean Baptiste Des Natchitoches was founded in the spring of 1714.

WILLIAM TELL (W.T.) LESTAGE★

William Tell (W.T.) Lestage, owner and manager of Lestage's Hardware and Appliances, Campti, La. He represents a 9th generation descendant in the Campti-Natchitoches area. Mr. Lestage wed Mary Catheryn Marcelli of Campti. Their children are: Catheryn Ann, who wed John Edward O'Shea of Tullos, La.; William Tell, Jr., and Robert Frank. Guierlero is Spanish for William. Guierlero Lestage was listed as a Natchitoches soldier in 1746.

GEORGE WASHINGTON LUCIUS

George Washington Lucius, Planter and Cotton Gin owner, wed Milinda Youngblood. His children were: Mecie Lucius, who wed Tal C. Gibson—Mattie Lucius who wed J. Henry Cain—James

W. Lucius who wed Sarah Pharis—Rupert L. Lucius who wed Laona Stone, Mr. Lucius was for many years Secretary and Treasurer of the Masonic Lodge at Fort Jesup, La. All of his children have added greatly to the economic welfare of Sabine Parish.

CHRISTOPHER C. McCAA★

Christopher C. McCaa wed Eunice La Cour of Natchitoches. They own and operate McCaa's Grocery at the junction of the Allen Road with Highway 6, one mile north of Robeline, La. This is just three tenths of a mile from the site of El Presidio Nuestra Senora del Pilar de Los Adais. Mrs. McCaa is always ready to assist visitors to the Los Adais area. This location was at one time a stage coach station on El Camino Real between Natchitoches and Fort Jesup.

Mrs. McCaa's family name, La Cour, appears very early in Natchitoches history. La Cour one of the fourteen French soldiers sent by St. Denis in 1723 to establish "Post du Rapides" which was the beginning of Alexandria, Louisiana. This post was established at the request of D'Artagnan, who was a direct envoy of King Louis XV, to Louisiana, and who later became known in French folklore as one of the Three Musketeers.

ARTHUR R. McCLERY

Arthur R. McClery, owner and manager of the P&C Drug at 116-122 Tuline street in Natchitoches, La., wed Theresa Hawkins of Parksdale, Ark. Their children are: Barbara Joan who wed Moreland Book (their children are Tina and David McClery Book), Patrica and Charlotte McClery. According to Breutin's map of 1722, the P&C Drug is located on the old original El Camino Real which entered Natchitoches on this street. This land was originally owned by Marichel and after the Louisiana Purchase the land was sold to Trudeau from whom Trudeau street is named. Mr. McClery has been one of the most successful men in Natchitoches, and has helped in the modern development of the Natchitoches-El Camino Real area.

GILES W. MILLSPAUGH

Giles W. Millspaugh, owner of Millspaugh's Drug at 576 Front St., wed to Ella Keener Charleville of Grosse Tete, La. Children are Giles W. Millspaugh, III, who wed Zora Lee Holloman, and Lelia Elizabeth who wed Floyd Allen Horton of Eunice, La. Mr. Millspaugh, a historian in his own right, has in one corner of his drug store, a history of Natchitoches in photographs and sketches. A must-stop for all who travel El Camino Real and who visit Natchitoches. Giles is Natchitoches' Front street historian and coin stamp collector. Mrs. Millspaugh, III, is from Winnfield, La.

CARSON MEADE NARDINI, SR.★

Carson Meade Nardini, Sr. of Alexandria, La. wed Pauline Marie Rand of Alco, La. Their children are: Joseph Hall, Carson Meade, Jr. and Alice Nanette. C. M. Nardini on his paternal grandparent's side is a descendant of Rouquier, Ballio, Chellettre, and Antoine Lassard who established Post Du Rapides. His is a descendant on his material grandparent's side of Rachal and Chellettre. His children represent 9th generation descendants in the Natchitoches-Alexandria area from 1723 to the present day.

LOUIS RAPHAEL NARDINI, JR.★

Louis Raphael Nardini, Jr., U. S. Army, being a descendant on his great grandmother's side of Possiot, is also a lineal descendant of Louis Badin. He represents an 8th generation descendant in the Natchitoches-El Camino Real area.

NATCHITOCHES BROADCASTING CO.
NORMAN FLETCHER-HILLMAN BAILEY, JR.

Located on the second floor of the Prudhomme-Hughes building is the voice of the Cane River area, K. N. O. C., the Natchitoches Broadcasting Co., owned and managed by Norman Fletcher and Hillman Bailey, Jr. Mr. Fletcher was educated in the Natchitoches Parish School System and is a graduate of Northwestern

State College in History and Journalism. He was selected as the Jaycee's of Natchitoches Man of the Year in 1958 and the Natchitoches Chamber of Commerce's Man of the Year in 1960. He is the first person to serve three consecutive years as President of the Chamber of Commerce in Natchitoches.

Mr. Hillman Bailey, Jr., President of the Natchitoches Broadcasting Co., a graduate of L.S.U. and a member of Delta Sigma Phi.

Mr. Bailey wed Terisa Zaunbrecher of Rayne, La. Their children are: Kathleen, Karl and David. Mr. Bailey is a descendant of Louis Chachere, an early settler of Opeolousas, La., and a descendant of the Bourbon family line.

ROLLIE EDWIN PATRICK

Rollie Edwin Patrick wed Miss Pearl Byrd of Florien, La. Their children are: Gerold E., who wed Bobbye Ruth Gregg of Charleston, S.C., Hubert Leroy who wed Marcie Ann Koch of Seattle, Wash.; Martha Ann, Periodical Librarian at McNeese College; Doris Lynelle, student at McNeese, and Betty Carolyn, Many High School student. Mr. Patrick's Service Station at the corner of San Antonio St. and the Shreveport Highway is an information stop for all tourists.

THE PERRIER FAMILY★

Of the union of Casimere Perrier and Marie Antoinette Rachal was Oscar Perrier, and of the union of Alexander Vercher and Natilie Gallion was Octavie Vercher who wed Oscar Perrier. Their children are: Oscar Joseph, Jr., James, Ruby John, Mable and Florence and Earney Grace, who wed James Mancheck of Nacogodoches, Tex. Their children are: Marlyn Ann, Janet Kay and Tammey Nell. The name "Perrier" is associated with Louisiana History as early as 1713 — in the Illinois Country, at Natchez and New Orleans.

ELMER LAWRENCE POCHE★

Elmer Lawrence Poche, Cloutierville, La. owners and manages Poche's Garage and Service Station, Highway 1, at Cloutierville.

He married Alice Brosset. Their children are: Elmer Lawrence, Jr., U.S.N.; Clara Calest who wed Donald Vercher (they have one child, Stephen Donald); Lynn Dale at N. S. College and Pauline Fay at Cloutierville High School. Mr. Poche is a descendent of the Lavespere family, and Mrs. Poche is a descendant of the Pierre Delouche family. They are 8th generation descendants in the Cloutierville-Natchitoches area.

WILLIAM A. PONDER

IN MEMORIAM

Taken from the monument of William A. Ponder, Fort Jesup, La.

"An extract from the resolution passed by the Democratic Central Executive Committee of the Parish of Natchitoches April 7, 1890, to-wit:

Resolved, that, whether as Chairman of this Committee, Member of the Legislature or Constitutional Convention, soldier or citizen, he was true to every trust, zealous in every duty, honest in every conviction, and he has left the legacy of an honest name. Unsullied by even the breath of calumny. Conspicuous in council for wisdom and moderation, farseeing and sagacious in the shaping of policies, courageous in the defense of the right—knowing no fear except to do wrong—he was once a safe leader and a successful public man.

To these characteristics he added those of a model Christian gentleman, a steadfast friend, kind father, loving husband and a pure exemplary life."

JAMES WOODROW PRUDHOMME★

James Woodrow Prudhomme, owner and manager of Sport-A-Pak on Highway 6 at the junction of the Grand Ecore-Campti, Highway. This business establishment dispenses all the necessary needs of the hunter or fisherman. Mr. Prudhomme is a 12th generation descendant of the Prudhomme listed on Breutin's map of 1722 of the Natchitoches area. James Woodrow Prudhomme wed Beatrice Thadis Black of Natchitoches. Their children are: James Larry, who attends N.S.C., and Catherine Diane who attends St. Mary's Academy.

RAY JOSEPH RAINES

Ray Joseph Raines, owner and manager of Raines General Store at Marthaville, La. wed Lillie Mae McCartney. Mr. Raines is a great nephew of J. J. Raines who founded Marthaville, La. His maternal grand father was John Spicher, a mess officer of the 7th U. S. Inf. who established Fort Jesup. Mr. Raines spearheaded the drive which successfully resulted in the establishment of the Marthaville Hospital, a community project.

STEPHEN CLYDE RAMBIN★

Stephen Clyde Rambin, owner and manager of Steves Texaco Service Station and Garage, Highway 1 at Powhattan, La. His father was Frank Louis Rambin and his mother Zelia Possiot. The family name, Rambin, is mentioned with St. Denis in 1713 and the Possiot name appears on Breutin's map of 1722. Stephen represents the 10th generation of the Rambin-Possiot union in the Natchitoches-Powhattan area. The Rambin family is well represented in the entire Ark.-La.-Tex. section.

MRS. ELAINE R. SMITH★

Mrs. Elaine R. Smith, neé Elaine Russell of Cypress, La., is Deputy Clerk of Court in Natchitoches, La. She is wed to Ellis Smith of Natchitoches, La. Mrs. Smith is a descendant of Thomas Vascoque, who is mentioned on another page. She is also a descendant of Armand who is mentioned in DeMezieres' report of 1769 on the merchants in Natchitoches.

RILEY JOHN (R.J.) STOKER

Riley John (R.J.) Stoker, Principal of Pleasant Hill High School, wed to Bernice Williams of Fair'View Alpha, La. They have one daughter, Revicca Ann who attends Louisiana Tech. Mr. Stoker is a fourth generation descendant of Henry Stoker who settled on land two miles from the present site of Fort Jesup in 1818. He gained extra land by trading ponies to the Indians. This Stoker, a leading member of the Citizens Committee, a vigilantes organization, assisted greatly in quelling the banditry of the Neutral Strip. He later supplied Fort Jesup with farm produce.

JOHN COLEMAN TARVER★

John Coleman Tarver, honorable Mayor of Many, La. wed Thelma Mayer of Woodward, Oklahoma. Their children are: Joan Tarver, who wed Wayne Dew of Natchitoches, La.; and Mike Thayne, senior at Many High School. Mayor Tarver owns and manages Tarvers' Grocery located on El Camino Real, which is Highway 6 east to Fort Jesup. Mr. Tarver is a descendant on his great grandmother's side of A. Cole who is listed in the 1806 period as being a settler in the Neutral Strip. Cole is also listed as a participant in the Guitreez-McGee Expedition to Texas in 1812.

THOMAS LESTER WARD

Thomas Lester Ward, owner of Ward's Esso Service Station and Garage at Robeline, La., wed Ellen E. Valentine of Jena, La. They have one son, Thermon Lester Ward who is an Electrical Engineer at Fort Worth, Texas. Mrs. Ward was an Elementary School Teacher at Jena and at Robeline. Ward's Service Station and Garage is located on El Camino Real in the Town of Robeline, La.

MRS. KENT WARDLOW★

Margaret Veuleman wed Kent Wardlow, President of the Bank of Montgomery, a member of the F.D.I.C. Their children are: Mary Ellen and Jennifer Ann. Mrs. Wardlow is a descendant of F. Veuleman who bought land from the firm of Smith, Baar, Davenport and Murphy in 1821 and marks the first purchase of land in what is presently the town of Many, La.

JACK EAZEL WHITLEY

Jack Eazel Whitley, owner of Whitley's General Store at Robeline, La. He married Ruby Alberta Nelson. There are these children: Ruby Marjorie who wed Stanley Ford Harvey of Shreveport, La. (they have one child, Stanley Ford, Jr.) ; Jack Eazel, Jr. wed Mary Alletta Coats of Marthaville, La. (their children are: Patricia Ann and David Van) ; Albert Jean, who wed Glenda Finell of Orange, Texas. (They have one child, Cynthia Jean) ; and Ruby Marjorie is a school teacher in Albuquerque, New Mexico, and Jack Eazel, Jr. is a dental technician in Shreveport, and Albert Jean is a chemist in Orange, Tex.

The father of Mr. Whitley, Sr., Andrew Jackson Whitley, owned the first butcher shop in the Robeline area.

Mr. Whitley Sr.'s second wife is Miss Ethyl Bates of Provencal, La. Mrs. Ethyl Bates Whitley taught school in Sabine Parish for a number of years.

MRS. IRMA SOMPAYRAC WILLARD

Irma Sompayrac Williard, neé Irma Rosalind Sompayrac, married David Milne Willard, Jr. of New York.

Their son: Daniel D. M. Willard, Lt. Cdr. U.S.N., married Suzanne Johnson of Arlington, Va., and their children are: Alice Darby, David Milne III, and Richard Briand of Virginia, Beach, Va.

Among forbears who served in the development of Natchitoches and of the state are Hon. Alexander E. Sompayrac who cast the deciding vote to abolish the Louisiana Lottery. His great-grand-father of Tarn, France, familiar with America through overseas trade and as a French naval officer, brought three sons to New Orleans via the West Indies. Ambrose married Desiree Josephine Briant, (daughter of a planter there and Colonel of a Regiment of French Dragoons, and Marie Mozard). Settling in Natchitoches about 1800, he bought new wireless telegraphy stock, using it in his cotton business. His place became a depot for trade with Mexico.

On the maternal side Alexandre Deblieux, dissenting from Napoleon, brought his sons from Provence and opened law and commission offices in New Orleans and Natchitoches where he planted cotton. One of his sons helped organize the first public parish school board. He married Euphrosine Tauzin of the Chamard family. His son married Julie, a daughter of Lestan Prud-homme, Sr. of the lines of Lambre, LeRoy, Philippe and Possiot. Mrs. Willard is the Supervisor of Art Education for the State of Louisiana.

Mrs. Lee Terry Williams

Mrs. Lee Terry Williams, neé Anna Louise Stille. Her home is located on the site of the John Baldwin Store of the 1826 period. On her father's side, Mrs. Williams is a lineal descendant of Princess Pocahontas and John Rolfe of early Virginia history. Through the families of Rolfe, Bolling, Mactin, Dr. W. B. Smith, Joseph Denning Stille, Sr., and Joseph Denning Stille, Jr., who was the father of Mrs. Lee Terry Williams.

Dr. William Kenneth Wimberly

Dr. William Kenneth Wimberly, dentist of Campti, La., wed Miss Bell Russel of Peason, La. Their daughter, Lynnie Ruth who is at present attending Natchitoches High School, was selected and honored as the Sweetheart of the Aircraft Carrier, Ranger. This old expression describes Dr. Wimberly perfectly: "a gentleman faultless in his carriage and deportment."

Marshall Ellis Winn

Marshall Ellis Winn, Planter and Rancher, Route 2 Robeline, La., wed Sadie Lenora Nims of East Orwell, Ohio. Their children are: James Jerold and Willard Allen, who wed Jacquelyn Beaver of Leesville, La. Their children are: Jacquelyn Ann, who attends Northwestern State College at Natchitoches, and Jimmy Jerold who attends High School in Alexandria. Mr. Winn was active in the organizing of the R.E.A. in Natchitoches and the adjoining Parishes. For 19 years he served as a Board Member in that organization.

Mrs. Sadie Winn taught in public schools 31 years at Robeline, La. Part of Mr. Winn's estate is part of Rancho Bano which was land alloted to the Mission, San Miguel de Cuellar de Los Adais, the profits of which were to support the Mission.

Glen Lawrence Wyatt

Glen Lawrence Wyatt, owner and manager of G. L. Wyatt's Esso Station at St. Maurice, La., wed Audrey Adams of Verda, La.

Their one son, George Miller, wed Sherley Anne Tacker of Segreves, Tex. When St. Denis and Bienville in 1700 were among the Yatasee Indians on Nantanchie Lake they would have also visited the Destonies Indians on Saline Bayou and then while enroute to the Natchitoches Indians, would have passed within 200 yards of Mr. Wyatt's business establishment. Both Mr. and Mrs. Wyatt are historians of this area.

www.ingramcontent.com/pod-product-compliance
Lightning Source LLC
Chambersburg PA
CBHW031256090426
42742CB00007B/484